PERFECT SUSPECT

a thrilling comedy

by

Robert Goodier

PERFECT SUSPECT

"Perfect Suspect"

Contact the author: Robbiegood@hotmail.com
robthewriter@hotmail.co.uk

ISBN : 978-1-4717-6627-5

First Published July 2012

Revised edition November 2012

OTHER PUBLISHED PLAYS BY THE AUTHOR

Murderous Intentions	ISBN 978-1-4709-3603-7
Ghost Of Thornley Hall In Cumbria	ISBN 978-1-4716-3653-0
Family Revelations	ISBN 978-1-2910-3231-4

POETRY BOOKS BY THE AUTHOR

Pin Number To the Real World	ISBN 0 9536748 0 0
Open Door Closed	ISBN 978-1-4478-2969-0
In The Third Person	ISBN 978-1-4716-3651-6

CONTENTS

Cast and scene list page 9

Perfect Suspect (the script) page 10

About the play page 64

Other plays by the author page 66

PERFECT SUSPECT

Cast of characters

MARCUS WINSTANLEY	Threatened by a 'voice from the past'.
AMANDA WINSTANLEY	Exasperated wife.
ALEXIS WINSTANLEY	Daughter, also threatened by the 'voice'
STUART WINSTANLEY	Brother, contests the will.
ALBERT FORSHAW	Family solicitor, with a dark secret.
DETECTIVE INSPECTOR TURNER	Desperate to solve a case.
DETECTIVE CONSTABLE GLOVER	The real brains of the two.

ACT ONE

SCENE ONE	Discovering the taped "threat".
SCENE TWO	One week later.
SCENE THREE	Ten days later.
SCENE FOUR	Two hours later.

ACT TWO

SCENE ONE	Two evenings later.
SCENE TWO	The "threat night".
SCENE THREE	Immediately after.

The action of the play takes place in the sitting room of Marcus and Amanda's home. The setting is the present day (or 25 years since cassette tapes were discontinued)

PERFECT SUSPECT Act One, Scene One.

As the curtains open, Marcus Winstanley is pacing up and down the room, deep in discussion with Albert Forshaw, the family solicitor, while Amanda his wife and Alexis, his daughter look on worried.

MARCUS I don't understand how it is possible! How could he see into the future? How could he know what would happen in my life? How it would turn out? How could he be so accurate?
ALBERT I don't know. Are you sure that it isn't a joke?
MARCUS How can I be sure of anything? I didn't even know that he held me with such high regard, let alone leave *me* with fourteen million pounds in his will. I hardly saw him other than birthdays and Christmas. Why would he leave me with so much money? And then say such horrible things about me on that tape?
ALBERT I cannot say.
MARCUS Oh come off it! You were his solicitor, surely he would have told you why!
ALBERT I merely followed his instructions, what more can I do?
MARCUS Well it is still peculiar and I don't like it. I fear for my family's safety. It isn't right that this should happen, not now while I have inherited his estate.
AMANDA I wouldn't take it seriously dear, it's most likely one of your uncle Henry's practical jokes.
MARCUS *(rounding on her)* Oh yes? And how come suddenly you are an expert on my uncle Henry? I hardly spoke of him to you and he wasn't the most pleasant of chaps. So come on, explain please.
AMANDA Your brother Stuart talks about him quite a lot.
MARCUS *(sneering)* Oh yes, Stuart. My brother who you see more than I do.
AMANDA Is that a problem? It's about time that you ended your stupid sulk with him and got back in touch with him.
MARCUS I will do no such thing! It is him who started this sulk and I am not going to be the one to talk to him until he talks to me first. It's a simple as that.
AMANDA Whatever you say dear, but this sulk has been going on for far too long don't you think?
MARCUS No, I don't. Why do you like him so much? What do you see in him that you don't see in me?
AMANDA I don't see anything in him, we only play squash together when we happen to be at the gym. He's quite a funny man. You should get to know again him and see the real Stuart.
MARCUS I have no intention of getting to know the 'real' Stuart, and neither should you. I think that it's high time you cancelled your membership of that gym.
AMANDA *(haughtily)* I will do no such thing! Anyway, this isn't the time to talk about your brother.
MARCUS No, you're right. I will drop it for now, but don't think that I'm going to forget it.

AMANDA Whatever, I'm not in the mood for arguing.
MARCUS Why not? You never seem to be in the mood for anything lately, except squash.
ALBERT Pardon me for interrupting, but don't you think the most important issue should be the tape?
MARCUS Yes. Yes of course. Quite correct Albert.
ALEXIS Do you think it could be joke daddy?
MARCUS I don't know. As your mother said, it could be. My uncle Henry was well known for his practical jokes. We'll have to wait for what the police say about the matter, they can "solve" this mystery.
ALBERT I don't want to cause any more friction between you and your brother sir, but could it be he who made the tape as revenge for you inheriting Henry's estate rather than him, or indeed, both of you? After all, he was closer to your uncle than you were.
MARCUS *(sarcastically)* Of course! My brother suddenly took it upon himself to 'threaten me' via a cassette! I've never heard anything so ridiculous Albert! My brother wouldn't even know how to programme his Sky plus box, let alone use a twenty five year old tape recorder! He's useless with technology, hasn't got the brains.
AMANDA *(rebuking)* Marcus! No need to talk to Albert like that! He was only suggesting something that's all.
MARCUS Even so, I don't know. It's not Stuart that's for sure. But good suggestion anyway Albert.
ALBERT Thank you sir.
MARCUS I don't understand it though. Henry was speaking to someone and what he said has come true. How can that be? Let's play the tape again.
ALBERT Are you sure sir?
MARCUS *(haughtily)* Of course I'm sure. Come on, play.

Albert presses play and the voice of Henry is heard, obviously talking to somebody else.

HENRY *(on tape)* I Henry Goodfellow proclaim this to be my last will and testament, dated the seventeenth of December nineteen eighty seven. Witnessed by my solicitor Michael Stevens. . . . .
ALBERT *(helpfully)* Who passed away five years ago.
MARCUS Yes, I know that! Shut up!
HENRY *(on tape, coughing)* I do not know how many years I have left. My illness comes and goes. It could be months, or years or I might pop off tomorrow. So here goes. Are you writing this down Michael?
MICHAEL *(on tape)* Well, no, it's being recorded.
HENRY Oh good grief man! Write it down, it's what you are being paid for! It isn't legal until it's written down you of all people should know that!
MICHAEL Sorry sir.
HENRY Now, my estate is to be divided the following way: my only remaining brother, Terence shall inherit all my properties, cars and house contents. My art

collection shall go to the museum, they've hounded me for long enough! My two bastard nephews, Stuart and Marcus who are the product of Terence being unfaithful to his wife, who I believe could not bear him children; I do not know as I am not particularly close to my brother or his wife; my two nephews will receive the following amounts: Stuart nothing – this is due to him being a raving mad homosexual. If you had expectations my boy – then tough! Marcus on the other hand, shall receive every penny I have. All my stocks and shares and the use of my nurse who is rather good at putting dressings on and gives a rather good bed bath. Good old Katrina – lovely girl, has two lovely assets of her own . . . .

Albert stops the tape.

MARCUS *(puzzled)* Why have you stopped the tape?
ALBERT I'm sorry sir, but haven't you heard the first part of the recording?
MARCUS So?
ALBERT Well, didn't you listen? All Henry's properties where to have been inherited by your father?
MARCUS So?
ALBERT But your father died eleven years ago. Therefore you inherit everything from your uncle Henry.
MARCUS Of course! *(jubilant)* Not only am I rich, but I have the choice of seven homes to live in across the world! Wow! What do you think my gorgeous girls?
AMANDA *(Shrugs)* Great.
ALEXIS Does this mean we could live in California for winter daddy?
MARCUS *(happily)* It certainly does! What's the matter with you Amanda? Aren't you pleased?
AMANDA I'll be pleased when this is all over.
MARCUS What do you mean? It's too good to be true don't you think? We're rich like lottery millionaires!
AMANDA Exactly, it's too good to be true. And why would your uncle say that Stuart is homosexual and wouldn't get anything – he's quite a womaniser.
MARCUS *(sarcastic)* Of course he is, that's why you play squash together.

Albert sensing hostilities resuming, cuts in.

ALBERT Shall we hear the rest of the tape?
AMANDA *(indifferent)* Oh please do.

Albert presses the play button. Henry's voice once again fills the room.

HENRY Now Marcus shall inherit my wealth on two conditions. Firstly he is to marry, preferably a woman and a stunning one at that and her name must begin with A, like my mother's; Amanda is a nice name and he must become a father before he is twenty, at the moment he is ten years old, so then his child must be at least sixteen for my inheritance to be claimed. And that child must be a son, if he is to have a girl

then the will is void and the money will go to my local dogs and cats home. But there is a way for Marcus to inherit my wealth and that is to either murder his daughter, or he be murdered as a result of his not bearing another child. Because I will know. If he has a boy then that's okay, the will stands. Now Michael, read back what I have just said. *(the tape stops)*
MARCUS I don't understand it. How could he know way back in nineteen eighty seven how my life would turn out? How did he know I would marry a woman by the name of Amanda and have a daughter? It doesn't make sense.
ALBERT You say you found this tape in that box filled with tapes that I gave to you?
MARCUS I did. There must be at least one hundred of them. I looked through them all to see if they were of interest and then I found that one – with my name on it.
ALBERT What were the other tapes? Any other peculiar ones?
MARCUS No, none. Mainly Jazz. Many of them were his own compilation tapes for the car and all of them dated. Some tapes went back to the early seventies.
ALBERT Well this tape certainly looks it's age. The label is tatty and the ink looks old. Until the police arrive we can only speculate.
MARCUS I don't know why the police have been called. This is simply a joke that's all. And our family affairs have nothing to do with a nosey plod asking lots of personal questions about us all. What will it prove anyway?
AMANDA It will clear the matter up, that's what. Your uncle only died three weeks ago. What's to say that he made that tape shortly before he died? That's how he knew so much about you and your brother.
MARCUS He hardly left his house in the last eight years of his life. I certainly didn't tell him about us and before you say it I know Stuart visited now and again to nurse him. So it only leaves Albert here who works for the solicitor – taking over from what's his name?
ALBERT Michael Stevens.
MARCUS So there was only Albert and Henry's many nurses who ever saw him on a regular basis. And Albert tells me that Henry was in very poor health the last few years of his life – barely able to speak. And also he was too weak to lift up a pen. So we have to assume one major thing I'm afraid.
ALBERT Oh? And what would that be sir?
MARCUS What is said on that tape is false. *(no response)* It has to be.
ALBERT Pardon me sir, but the last will your uncle made *was* in nineteen eighty seven. He never renewed it. So I think I can safely assure you of its authenticity.
MARCUS Okay, I'll believe that. For now. But I am not touching a penny of it until I know what is going on. This whole tape thing is too freaky for me.
ALBERT As you wish sir.

The doorbell rings.

ALEXIS That will be the police. Can I go daddy?
MARCUS Certainly.

Alexis skips out of the room. Amanda rises, moving to drinks cabinet.

AMANDA Anybody want one?
MARCUS *(not impressed)* Do you think it's wise with a plod coming through the door any second? We don't want the smell of Glenfiddich on our breath do we?
AMANDA *(pouring herself one)* What does it matter? This our house, the police have only come to give you peace of mind. Quite frankly, I say they're a bad idea. But I'm your wife – so what do I know?
ALBERT The police are involved because of the death threat that has been made towards your husband and your daughter. I thought it a prudent precaution – that is all.
AMANDA *(sarcastic)* Well done Jeeves, very commendable I must say!

Alexis bounds in with two very serious looking women who take in the room with their trained air of suspicion. One of them fixes her eyes on Marcus.

TURNER Mister Marcus Winstanley I presume? (*holds out her hand to shake)*
MARCUS *(shakes her hand)* I am, this is my wife, Amanda, my daughter Alexis and Albert Forshaw, who is the executer of my uncles estate.
TURNER Pleased to meet you. I am Detective Inspector Turner and this is my colleague Detective Constable Glover.
MARCUS Thank you for coming, I didn't expect plain clothes officers, I expected a uniform to investigate. I must say you are not the policeman looking type.
TURNER And what did you expect? Morse and Lewis? Inspector Barnaby? Cagney and Lacy? Starsky and Hutch?
MARCUS Well I don't know about Starsky and Hutch and I don't know who Barnaby is; but Morse and Lewis most certainly.
TURNER Yes, well we often get that. It's about time that Joe Public realised that there are high ranking policewomen in the force. It's not all beer swilling down the pub for us you know.
MARCUS I do apologise for my misplaced perception.
TURNER That's quite alright sir, no harm done. Now, who rung the police about a death threat?
ALBERT That would be me.
TURNER I see. And who would you be?
ALBERT I am Albert Forshaw, family solicitor, to the er, family.
TURNER So mister Forshaw, can you tell us what this 'death threat' consists of. Is it a letter?
ALBERT No, it is on a tape that Mister Marcus Winstanley found whilst clearing out his uncles effects.
TURNER I see. Is this cassette with you now?
ALBERT It is.
TURNER May we hear it?
ALBERT Certainly. It will need rewinding, give me a moment please.

He busies himself with rewinding the tape.

TURNER Not a problem. Now, who is the 'death threat' made towards?
MARCUS To me.
ALEXIS And me daddy!
MARCUS And you too, sorry dear.
TURNER Who was this threat made by?
MARCUS Actually, by my deceased uncle Henry.
TURNER *(surprised)* Your deceased uncle Henry? When did he die?
MARCUS Three weeks ago. The last ten years of his life he was bed bound, he just wasted away.
GLOVER Did you see him often in that period sir?
MARCUS Good grief no! Not for his last five years at least! I couldn't stand the smell! He was using his bed as a toilet and the whole house just hummed of death. God lord, no.
TURNER That sounds rather heartless sir.
MARCUS Well I suppose it does now I've said it out loud. But the stench was like twenty old people in a home, it was unbearable!
ALBERT *(timely)* The tape is ready to play now.
TURNER Good, play it please.

Albert complies and the recording is heard in its entirety, but he stops it at the point when Henry says 'read back what I've just said'. D.I. Turner muses over what she's heard.

TURNER Is that it?
ALBERT It is.
TURNER Interesting. Very interesting.
MARCUS *(aghast)* Is that all you can say? My life has been threatened, my daughter's life has been threatened. What can you do?
TURNER Well sir, it sounds like a practical joke to me.
MARCUS You wouldn't joke if you knew that a lot of what he said has come true! I married a woman called Amanda and I have a daughter – Alexis, not a son. So how could he know these facts from so long ago?
TURNER That I cannot say sir. I would need to take this tape away for examination, would that be okay with you?
MARCUS Yes of course, do what you have to do.
TURNER I will have a copy made for you. This original we will have to keep as evidence.
MARCUS Do what you have to do, but find the perpetrator as soon as you can, my life and my daughter's life is at stake here.
TURNER Yes, of course. Now I need to establish the origin of this tape. How did you come by it?
MARCUS I received a box from Henry's solicitors two weeks ago. I didn't give it a thought because I was so busy. Anyway, one night, out of boredom, I decided to open

it. It had on it a rather cheap new looking padlock, but that didn't matter as I was given the key to it, it was on my key ring funnily enough. Anyway, when I opened it I was expecting treasure, or something like it, so I was disappointed to see that it was jammed full of old cassettes. Anyway, I looked through them all in the hope that something might be worth listening too, but they were all his collection of jazz music – which I hate, I must say. And then suddenly I came across this cassette with my name on it. So, being intrigued I played it and it is the tape that you have just heard.

TURNER It is indeed intriguing. So are you sure it is your uncles voice on that recording? Could it be someone else do you think?

MARCUS Well as far as I can remember it does sound like him. But, as I said, I never really saw him in his later years, but it does sound like him. Actually, Albert here knew him better than I, ask him.

GLOVER So mister Forshaw, how well did you know Henry, Marcus's uncle?

ALBERT Very well, I am employed by the solicitors to execute his will. I was with him nearly every day for three years until he died.

GLOVER Did you have any knowledge of this taped death threat before Marcus Winstanley first heard it?

ALBERT None. Until it was first played to me a few days ago I didn't even know of its existence.

MARCUS Do you think it's worth following up on?

TURNER *(grandly)* I certainly do. But I will have to speak to my ops commander, what with the cut backs and everything, but I would certainly like to pursue this as it intrigues me. In fact, even if he says no, I will investigate. A voice from the dead predicting your life? Fascinating stuff!

MARCUS (*relieved)* Oh thank you. Thank you so much!

He takes Turners, then Glovers hand and shakes them vigorously.

TURNER *(pleasantly surprised)* Well thank you sir. We will do our very best to solve this case.

MARCUS *(pleased)* I know you will.

TURNER Tell me more about Henry Goodfellow.

MARCUS Well, he's a millionaire, he earned his money through banking and he owns, sorry, *owned,* a large regional bank that was bought out by Barclays about sixteen years ago; he stayed on as CEO. He owns several properties around the world and owns a substantial art portfolio. His total wealth is somewhere around fourteen million pounds, not counting his properties and art collection.

GLOVER I see, so that is what you will inherit as the last known relative of his, that is quite a substantial amount of money.

MARCUS It is, especially as my job is a Home Office advisor to the Government, it makes me a high risk target for such threats as this.

AMANDA Don't forget Stuart, Marcus.

GLOVER Stuart?

MARCUS My brother.

GLOVER Your brother, sir?

MARCUS Yes, my brother. I haven't seen him in eight years, but I am sure I will now with all this Will business.
TURNER Of course, so he will also gain from Mister Goodfellow's passing. *(to Albert)* Mr Forshaw, is there a written will of this tape somewhere at your solicitors that will confirm what Mr Goodfellow dictated to. . . . ?
ALBERT Michael Stevens, Miss.
TURNER I am a senior officer, I am addressed as 'ma'am'.
ALBERT *(embarrassed)* Well 'ma'am', I think that there most certainly be one. I will endeavour to look as soon as I can.
TURNER Good, good. Well mister Winstanley, if there is indeed a written transcript of the will dated the same as what we have heard on the tape, then that, with unquestionable clarity, will prove that this tape is genuine.
MARCUS Excellent! That is good news *(to Amanda)* isn't it darling?
AMANDA *(yawning)* It is.
MARCUS *(shocked)* No need to be so enthusiastic about it. What do you think Alex?
ALEXIS *(pleased)* It is indeed good news father.
MARCUS *(happily)* Great! *(to Turner and Glover)* Now, would you two like a cup of tea or coffee?
GLOVER Ooh, tea please. No sugar.
MARCUS And you. . . . ?
TURNER *(embarrassed)* Actually, may I please use your loo? I've been holding it for the last three hours and I'm really in desperate need.
AMANDA *(shocked, but polite)* Yes of course, it's upstairs, second door on left.
TURNER *(relieved)* Many thanks, much appreciated.

She suddenly bolts out of the room, everyone looks on, stunned.

GLOVER Oh don't you worry, she's always like this, weak bladder you see. But the trouble is – many people actually think that she is taking the pi . . . . .
MARCUS *(hurriedly interrupting)* Two sugars was it?
GLOVER *(confused)* No sir, none.

The mood becomes tense and strained, finally Amanda breaks it.

AMANDA Have you been a policewoman long Glover?
GLOVER *(confused)* No, but I would give it ten minutes if I was you.
MARCUS *(puzzled)* Pardon?
GLOVER Sorry sir, I thought your wife was referring about another matter.

She smiles, though obviously confused.

END OF SCENE ONE

SCENE TWO A week later.

Marcus and Alexis are relaxing. Marcus is reading a Jeffrey Archer novel, Alexis is flicking through the TV channels, bored.

ALEXIS Daddy, can I ask you something?
MARCUS *(not looking up)* Certainly dear.
ALEXIS Well, it's about that tape your uncle Henry made.
MARCUS What about it?
ALEXIS Well, it's what he said on it. How could he know what you would do with your life from so long ago?
MARCUS I don't know sweetheart. But what I do know is the two policewomen will solve it, that I am certain of.
ALEXIS They might be able to solve it, but your life has been threatened and so has mine. How can you be so relaxed about it?
MARCUS *(amazed)* Relaxed? You think I am relaxed? Has it escaped your attention that I haven't left this house since the police left here with the tape? I am not venturing outside until I have the all clear. And neither are you.
ALEXIS *(protesting)* Dad, that's not fair! I haven't seen my boyfriend Richard for nearly a month now. It's not fair! Why do I have to stay in?
MARCUS Because it's not safe for you to go out. How many more times do you have to be told?
ALEXIS *(protesting)* But dad!
MARCUS *(firmly)* But nothing! If he is so important to you then he can come here to you. But no staying over, do you here? And who is this Richard anyway?
ALEXIS Awe dad! I'm nearly eighteen you know, it's not like I'm a kid is it?
MARCUS No it's not. But I don't want him staying over. For one, where would he sleep?
ALEXIS In the spare room. *(smugly)* Like he has done many times before.
MARCUS *(shocked)* Pardon?
ALEXIS He's stayed over loads of times before dad and nothing 'happened'. Much.
MARCUS *(puzzled)* When?
ALEXIS All those times you stayed away on 'business' last year.
MARCUS *(realises)* I was away at least twelve times. . . . and your mother let you?
ALEXIS She did. Unlike you dad, she's not a prude.
MARCUS *(shocked)* Did you co-habit?
ALEXIS *(puzzled)* Did we what?
MARCUS Share a bed? *(Alexis giggles, Marcus is furious. Amanda enters and sits aside the annoyed Marcus)* Did you know our daughter was sleeping with her boyfriend in our house all the times I was away?
AMANDA Of course I did. She's seventeen, nearly eighteen. She is legal age, what's the problem?
MARCUS *(shocked)* What's the problem? I'll tell you what the problem is, what if she got pregnant, that's what the problem is! She's barely seventeen and you let her 'boyfriend' sleep in her bed! I am totally shocked! I'm speechless, I . . .

AMANDA I think you should shut up, that's what I think.
MARCUS Really? So if she got pregnant who would be the bad parent? You or me?
ALEXIS Dad, I am in the room you know. I won't get pregnant because I am on the pill and Richard is very careful you know.
MARCUS *(stunned)* I don't want to know any more young lady!
AMANDA *(amused)* Don't worry dear, your father is shocked because he was eighteen before he had his first sexual encounter, you've just beaten him by two years *(winks)* and that was with me.
MARCUS *(embarrassed)* Do you mind talking about my sex life so intimately in front of our daughter?
AMANDA *(teasing)* Oh don't be such a prude. How would you like it if Alex did become pregnant and you are suddenly a thirty something grandfather? She is actually quite liberated, you could learn a lot from her.
MARCUS *(huffing)* I would rather not. I would feel extremely humiliated being given sex education lessons by my seventeen year old daughter.
ALEXIS *(proudly)* I love him dad and we are going to get married and you can't stop it.
MARCUS Maybe not and yes, you are right, I cannot stop you. But I don't remember this Richard lad. Who is he?
ALEXIS *(amazed)* Oh come on dad, you know who he is. He won the school talent show last year. That's when you first met him.
MARCUS *(remembering)* Oh yes, I know who you mean. Wasn't he the young chap who did impersonations?
ALEXIS He's an impressionist dad.
MARCUS What's the difference? It's still a funny voice at the end of the day.
ALEXIS Whatever dad. Yes, he does funny voices and for your information, he has reached the regional heats in "Search for A Voice".
AMANDA Well done Richard! High five! (*Alexis and Amanda high five, while Marcus pulls his face and shrugs).*
ALEXIS I saw that dad. Do you know what "Search for a voice" is?
MARCUS Some kind of cheapskate X Factor?
ALEXIS Nearly. It's a showcase for new comedians who have a five minute slot to impersonate celebrities. It's great, Richard has got to the semi finals!
MARCUS *(not impressed)* Well whoopee do!
ALEXIS *(angrily)* Dad! Don't be so dismissive will you, if he wins it could lead onto great things for him you know!
MARCUS Well, as I do not know this Richard I think I can detach myself away from your obvious biased hysteria. It would have been nice to have been introduced to him; but no! You chose to keep him a secret from me. How do you think I feel about it? So I will bid him good luck, but as you and your mother found it best to keep him a secret from me then I will not get involved. It's as simple as that.

Alexis runs from the room in tears, Marcus tuts, Amanda rebukes him.

AMANDA Subtle as usual.

MARCUS Well . . . . why should I give a monkeys about her boyfriend's so called 'success'? I've never met him, in fact until five minutes ago I didn't know of his existence. Oh just leave me alone won't you!
AMANDA You really are heartless aren't you? Alexis talks nothing else but Richard, you don't listen to her.
MARCUS I do listen! I just filter out what is important from the rubbish she spouts, that's all.
AMANDA So our daughters romance is 'rubbish'? Is that it?
MARCUS No, not at all. I just don't feel comfortable talking to her about that sort of stuff. That's more your thing and you are extremely good at it.
AMANDA *(sneers)* You wimp.
MARCUS I am a man, I have never been given lessons in how to be a parent.
AMANDA And neither have I. You know, if you are not careful, Alexis will be married and have children before you realise what has happened, so it is in your best interests to keep your eyes open you know.
MARCUS Well if she does, then she will not go short with the money that I've inherited from uncle Henry. I will make sure her children have the finest education and all the toys that they can play with.
AMANDA *(sarcastically)* Well aren't you the generous one.
MARCUS I don't see why not. What's wrong with giving them a good start in life?
AMANDA Nothing. But you change your mind as often as your underwear.
MARCUS What do you mean? I change my underwear at least four times a week.
AMANDA Exactly!
MARCUS Ahh, I get it, its insult Marcus day is it?
AMANDA Yes.

The doorbell sounds.

MARCUS Saved by the bell.
AMANDA Of course dear, lucky you.
MARCUS Why are you being such a bitch lately? It's like you don't care about the death threat towards me and Alexis.
AMANDA *(indifferent)* Well, I am bothered, sorry if I don't seem to care about you.
MARCUS Thank you.

A serious looking Inspector Turner and Detective Constable Glover enter, Alexis follows then in, closing the door.

TURNER Good afternoon Mister Winstanley, Mrs Winstanley.
AMANDA Good afternoon.
MARCUS *(standing)* Yes, good afternoon. I take it this is not a social call?
TURNER Correct sir.
ALEXIS Is it about the tape?
GLOVER It is miss. There has been a further development. You had better sit down and you sir.

MARCUS *(worried)* What could it be?
TURNER Did you play the tape any further than the section you played to us when we first arrived?
MARCUS No I didn't. There didn't seem to be any point. Why?
TURNER Well sir *(she produces an A4 sized folder and hands out three sheets of paper)* There was a lot more spoken by your uncle after the section you played to us. This is a transcript. Unfortunately we cannot play the actual recording to you as it is now evidence in a possible murder plot against you and your daughter.
MARCUS *(Shocked)* What?
GLOVER Please read the transcript sir. It's all there.

Marcus reads through it, his face ashen. He takes Alexis hand and squeezes it. She is equally scared.

MARCUS *(puzzled)* I don't understand. There was a third person in the room?
TURNER Yes sir, it appears so.
MARCUS It says here that this third person has been asked by my uncle to "bump us off" and they are agreeing a price?
TURNER It does, correct sir. As stated it is because and I quote from the transcript, "if he doesn't produce a son in the first five years of his marriage, or he has a daughter, then he must be dealt with as soon as possible and so must the daughter. I am not having my money going to waste on a girl. No way. So how much will it cost"? That is your uncle speaking. The reply from the third person is thus: "forty grand for the man and thirty for the girl. If you want them bumped off at the same time I'll do it for sixty grand". To which your uncle replies "deal".
GLOVER Are you certain that you never heard this section of the tape before sir?
MARCUS *(worried)* No, never. It was always stopped it at the same point. There didn't seem much point in listening any further, as far as I was concerned, it said all it needed and I took that to be a threat in itself. Or rather Albert Forshaw did.
TURNER We have been trying to contact Mr Forshaw for the last three days. Do you know of his whereabouts?
MARCUS No I don't. He's the family solicitor, he doesn't live with us you know.
TURNER Have you spoken to him in the last week at all?
MARCUS No, the last time I saw him was the day you two arrived. Do you think it could be him?
TURNER Well sir, I wouldn't like to speculate anything at this stage. But he is your solicitor and he also works for the firm that your uncle left his Will with.
MARCUS Would there be any chance of me having the tape back?
GLOVER None sir, but as I said on our first meeting, you can have a copy. The lab boys are analysing it.
MARCUS Why? What do they hope to find?
GLOVER Well it's all very technical, but basically they listen for any obscure background noises or strain in the voice to work out if your uncle was under pressure to say what he said. Also they can determine the age of the cassette, whether it was manufactured around nineteen eighty seven or before.

MARCUS *(impressed)* Really? And the lab boys can do all that can they?
GLOVER Oh yes sir, you'd be surprised what can be done with modern technology nowadays.
MARCUS *(impressed)* Incredible.
TURNER Well sir, we must get back to the station. At some point in the next week or so we will need to chat to both you and your daughter – separately – regarding this death threat. Don't worry, you are not suspects, it is just to establish whether you have enemies or there are people who may have a grudge that you have come into so much money and therefore wish to cause you problems. Strictly a formality, you understand?

Alexis is worried.

GLOVER *(soothingly)* No need to look so worried young lady, we'll protect you, you won't come to any harm I assure you. Good day to you all.

They move to exit. Amanda, who has been reading the transcript stops them.

AMANDA Hang on, hang on. Marcus, you haven't read this through and you two either 'forget' to mention it, or you are not as concerned for my families well-being as you like to make out.
TURNER *(puzzled)* Why is that Mrs Winstanley?
AMANDA Uncle Henry names the day for my husband and daughter to be killed. It is the twenty fourth of this month!
TURNER *(remembering)* Ahh, yes, I knew there was another reason for us being here.
MARCUS *(shocked)* What?! *(snatches transcript from her)* You're right, it does! That's two weeks away! How could you forget about this 'tiny' detail?
TURNER *(shrugs)* Ahh, yes, there was another matter, Glover, how did you forget to mention it?
GLOVER *(shocked)* Me ma'am? I er. . .
TURNER *(embarrassed)* Never mind. Yes Mrs Winstanley, well spotted.
AMANDA Well spotted my backside! You forgot didn't you? I'm beginning to wonder if you two are capable in your capacity of police officers to protect my husband and daughter of this death threat.
TURNER No need to be offensive madam. It was simply overlooked, that is all.
AMANDA *(not convinced)* Really? What is the direct line number to your superior officer? Let me speak to him or I shall put in an official complaint.
TURNER *(suddenly pleading)* Oh please no, don't do that! I need this case, I really do!
AMANDA *(stunned)* Pardon? What are you saying?
MARCUS *(stunned)* Yes, please explain yourselves. What do you mean by you 'need this case'?
TURNER It's quite simple Mr Winstanley; my immediate superior is going to have me demoted to Detective Constable and Glover here will be back on traffic duty

unless we come up with a 'solved case'. My track record isn't good in the three years I've been a D.I. And I need this case, it could be the one that keeps me a D.I.

AMANDA *(amazed)* Are you telling us that we have Laurel and Hardy solving my families death threat? My god! What kind of police officers do they employ nowadays?

TURNER *(defensively)* I am not *incompetent* Mrs Winstanley, I did not become a poor officer overnight you know.

MARCUS *(scoffing)* Really? Well you will just have to prove it to us. And if I do end up being assassinated you will find yourself off the case and other more 'competent' officers will investigate. In fact, come to think of it, we only took your word that you are police officers, you didn't show us your warrant cards and collar numbers.

TURNER Very well, if that is all it takes. Come on Glover, get yours out. *(Both of them show their warrant cards.)*

MARCUS Well, they looks genuine enough to me. But if you don't mind, I will ring your station to confirm your identities. May also I have your unique warrant numbers please and the station you are seconded too.

Humiliated, Turner and Glover let Marcus take down the details he needs.

Thank you. Central Station eh? Then the top ranking officer there is Chief Superintendent Alan Lancaster, a very good golf friend of mine. Now, I am sure you will understand that until I receive official confirmation that you really are police officers, it would be best if you leave my house. You understand don't you?

TURNER Perfectly. It is so very wise to be cautious. Come on Glover, let's go.

MARCUS *(annoyed)* Show them out will you Alex.

ALEXIS *(happily)* Certainly father.

She ushers out the hapless pair. Marcus looks at Amanda baffled.

MARCUS *(puzzled)* Well, what do you make of that?

AMANDA Very strange. I had a funny feeling about them from the off. I've never known of plain clothed policewomen before. I mean, I've seen them on the television, but I never knew there really were actual *real* ones.

MARCUS Real incompetent ones at that! How could they forget about the date of my murder? Surely that would have been the most important piece of news I should have been told about. Let me look at that transcript. *(skims through it)* Well, there it is, twenty fourth of this month. That's fourteen days away. I really don't understand how this can be? Did uncle Henry have special powers to see into the future? It's incredible!

AMANDA I doubt it.

MARCUS *(surprised)* Really? Please explain.

AMANDA Oh I will. It's a fake.

MARCUS *(aghast)* I said that last week when we first heard it, but you laughed at me. So now *you* say it – well wow! It really is “a fake”! Well thank you Miss Marple!

AMANDA No need to be like that!

MARCUS Why not? We actually agree about something, that must be a first as we haven't agreed on anything in years.

AMANDA That maybe, don't get so carried away. And another thing, I think Albert is in on it, because he never played the tape past the point when Henry says "read back what I've just said". So the police should look at him as the number one suspect.

MARCUS *(amazed)* Albert? Never. And although I do think it is good theory you are wrong in one respect.

AMANDA Oh yes? And what would that be?

MARCUS Well, it was me who stopped the tape at that point. I never played it any further when I let Albert hear it, so I am the one to blame really. I was so shocked when I heard what I heard, it never occurred to me to play it any further and Albert on hearing the section that he heard insisted on phoning the police. So in effect all this mess is my fault.

AMANDA Oh dear, I can understand the shock, but we only heard four minutes of what is a nine minute recording.

MARCUS I know, I know. But what do I do? Everything on that tape has come true; from the point of view when it was recorded, so the big question is – how did he *know* how my life was going to turn out? And why leave me, as his last known relative such a huge amount of money and *then* leave that tape? It doesn't make sense.

AMANDA Well, if Pinky and Perky can solve it your mind will soon be at rest.

MARCUS And that is another thing. Detective Turners strange outburst. Something isn't right there either.

AMANDA I think so too. But a call to their police station will confirm if they are 'real police' or imposters.

MARCUS Why do you say 'imposters'?

AMANDA Well, we don't know how many other 'relatives' of yours are still around. Maybe they are distant relatives who have just found out about your inheritance and have come to 'suss you out' as it were.

MARCUS *(stunned)* And how would they do that?

AMANDA Internet. Simple as that. They log on to 'obituary websites', discover the death of your uncle; think 'bloody hell, the old git didn't leave us a penny'. Then they 'pretend' to be police officers in order to find out more about you.

MARCUS And how does Albert fit into all this? Is he a relative and contacted Turner and Glover when he discovered how the will was going to be distributed and they all hatched a plan to somehow get it from me by making a tape?

AMANDA Well stranger things happen in films you know.

MARCUS *(scoffing)* A ridiculous idea! Why did you ever give up writing children's story's I'll never know!

AMANDA *(annoyed)* I gave up writing children's books because I had a child! A fact that you conveniently forget from time to time! You are always away on business, you've hardly seen her grow up and you have never shown any interest in what she is doing! Do you realise how upsetting it is for her?

MARCUS *(puzzled)* Hang on, how has Alexis come into the argument?

AMANDA She is always the argument as far as I am concerned! I've brought her up practically on my own as you were never here and when you were here did you involve yourself with her? No, you didn't. Why do you think she was upset when she told you about Richard and how proud she is of him? She loves him and she's happy, but you dismiss him because you have 'never met him'. Is it any wonder that she doesn't tell you anything about what she does with her life?

MARCUS What? Like him staying over for the night and sharing her bed?

AMANDA *(firmly)* She is nearly eighteen years old.

MARCUS Oh and that makes things alright does it?

AMANDA She is happy with him.

MARCUS So? And that makes things A-ok does it? Sharing a bed, staying over? She isn't mature enough to know what she is doing and quite frankly I think it is wrong.

AMANDA You do, do you? Well let me tell you this Marcus; since this 'death threat' you have actually stayed in this house for nine straight days. A record.

MARCUS And it will be a bigger record than nine days, because I am not leaving this house until I get the all clear from the police and whoever made that threat has been found and locked away. So you and Alex had better get used to me being around a lot more from now on.

AMANDA Well that won't work will it? Because the threat was made from your uncle Henry who is now dead, so the police will have a fair bit of paper work trying to get a stiff into Risley won't they?

MARCUS *(stunned, beat)* Sometimes I really don't know you, you know.

AMANDA And whose fault is that?

MARCUS Oh I can't be bothered with arguing. I'm going to bed to read.

AMANDA *(surprised)* Really? It's only eight o'clock.

MARCUS Well if I'm being honest – it's to get away from you.

AMANDA *(annoyed)* And that's been your solution to everything lately hasn't it? Going to bed early won't solve anything you know!

MARCUS Maybe not, but it gets me away from you for the night. See you.

AMANDA Sleep tight won't you with all that money stuffed into the mattress.

MARCUS *(sarcastic)* Oh I just love your sarcasm.

AMANDA Of course you do, that's why you married me in the first place because of my humour.

MARCUS You're right and the trouble is the humour keeps coming as you have the last laugh should I ever decide to divorce you.

AMANDA I should say so. Seven million of them to be exact.

MARCUS Yes well, no need to be so smug you know. If I do get bumped off then you're looking at twice that.

AMANDA Plus interest, don't forget.

MARCUS Yes, well, let's hope that it doesn't come down to that. *(exits)*

AMANDA *(pours a large drink, muses)* Fourteen million pounds. Wow Marcus, if that tape does come true then you've made me a very happy rich woman. Cheers.

END OF SCENE TWO

SCENE THREE Ten days later.

Stuart has arrived, he is sat on the armchair, Marcus is pouring two drinks, he hands one to Stuart and sits down in the armchair opposite. They are both awkward and stand offish to each other.

MARCUS Well Stuart, it's been quite a few years. Thank you for coming round to see me to discuss this will of uncle Henry's.
STUART *(unhappy)* Yes, well, believe me, I didn't want too, it was Samantha who insisted that I came to see you, if it was up to me I would quite happily not see you for another eight years.
MARCUS Same here, Amanda also insisted that we talk. *(reluctantly)* So, how have you been?
STUART *(sarcastically)* How do you mean? In general? In life? In health?
MARCUS Now don't be awkward Stuart, you know what I mean. What do you expect me to ask you after so long?
STUART Of course, you're right, I'm sorry. *(smiles)* I've been well, my health is good, my life is good, I travel the world, eat good food, have a fantastic family, a drop dead gorgeous wife and everything is tickety boo. How about you?
MARCUS Much the same as you. I'm working hard, the job is more than I could ever want and things are going well. Apart from this will and death threat business.
STUART Yes, the will and the death threat. Don't you think that it is all a bit far-fetched?
MARCUS It could be, but I am not taking any chances, that's why the police are involved and why I am not returning to my post until I get the all clear.
STUART Ah yes, the post. How is the job going? The one that you stole from me.
MARCUS I didn't steal any post from you. I was never aware that you had applied for the post, just as you didn't know that I had. You knew the protocols at the time. But storming out of the restaurant was a bit childish don't you think?
STUART Not really. It was your smug announcement on my birthday that did it for me. It was like you stabbed me in the back.
MARCUS *(angrily)* Don't be so stupid! At least you left after you ate that very expensive steak, that's something I suppose.
STUART Well maybe I was being "stupid" at the time and looking back on it perhaps it was "stupid", but what annoyed me over the years was the fact that you never, in the last eight years, never once asked me how I was. You never rang me, enquired about me – it was like you had totally given up on me.
MARCUS *(scoffing)* So you are blaming me for the fact that we haven't spoke for so long now are you? You could just as easily rang me to find out how I am doing, but you didn't; so we are both childish don't you think? And you say I "stole" your potential Government post and "rubbed your nose in it", as well as ignoring you?
STUART Yes. *(sarcastic)* How is the job going? Pay well does it?
MARCUS *(proudly)* I can't complain, eighty grand a year, I tour the world, stay in the best hotels. . . .
STUART *(clapping)* Whoopee doo! Well I too have a new job, been in it a year and I

also travel the world and stay in the best hotels.

MARCUS *(sarcastic)* Oh yes, Amanda told me, aren't you a tractor parts salesman?

STUART *(annoyed)* And what is wrong with that?

MARCUS *(dismissively)* Nothing, it's a job I suppose.

STUART *(angrily)* No need to be snotty about it!

MARCUS I'm not being snotty, a tractor parts salesman is better than nothing.

STUART Forty grand a year is more than “nothing” and it is a great job and I am not ashamed of it.

MARCUS I never said it was anything to be ashamed of, don't be so touchy will you. It is good that you are working and it is also good that we are talking to each other isn't it?

STUART Yes well, if this will business hadn't happened we would probably still be ignoring each other and as you say, we are talking now and that is good, don't you think?

MARCUS Yes, it is and thank uncle Henry for our reunion, he is the “peacemaker” shall we say? His estate could be the thing we need to become brothers again, don't you think?

STUART *(mocking)* “Don't you think? Don't you think”? Have you heard yourself? Well I'm not having it! Why would uncle Henry leave *you* his entire estate and not me? You never went anywhere near him in his last few years, it was always me! And this so called 'tape of death' is nonsense! I've never heard of something so ridiculous in my life and you, as my stupid brother has fallen for it! It is a trick obviously perpetrated by uncle Henry, or someone near him to discredit me calling me a 'homosexual' and you *actually believe* it! My god Marcus, how gullible you are!

MARCUS How can you say that? You've heard the tape, you say it sounds like uncle Henry, so it must be true.

STUART You have always been dense haven't you? That tape is false, it isn't true. Somebody made that tape to discredit me from the will and has done a good job. Now we know there is a will written from nineteen eighty seven as it was read out verbally on that tape. That, as far as I am concerned is the *true* will. And I doubt that too. Henry must have made another will before he died. None of this makes any sense to me. That tape proves nothing, it could be anything. It could be Henry just playing one of his jokes or it could be just plain false. Have the police come up with anything?

MARCUS Not yet. But I do wish they would hurry up. If that tape is real then Alexis and I have only four days left to live and all Henry's money goes to his local dogs and cats home and his properties and effects will just got to ruin and I can't have that, it seems such a waste.

STUART And that is why I am contesting his will. It doesn't seem to me that you have investigated this at all due to the pound signs in your eyes. You go off a taped recording without real proof that it was recorded by Henry and you drag the police into our affairs. As my older brother I thought you had a lot more reason to be cautious over such a matter of fourteen million pounds. But as I say, you were blinkered, that was all you could see.

MARCUS *(annoyed)* No it was not! I didn't expect that amount and I definitely would have shared it equally with you!

STUART *(scoffing)* Yeah right.

MARCUS Yes I would! And you know it too.

STUART So you waited for me to come back from my holiday in the Caribbean to tell me the 'good news' of uncle Henry's death? My god Marcus, you're pathetic!

MARCUS Whoa, hang on here. Why should I tell you about it and spoil your holiday? Plus the fact that number one; I didn't know you were on holiday and secondly; we haven't spoken to each other for nearly eight years! Or has that simple fact escaped what passes for a brain in your head nowadays? The trouble with you is that you just don't think do you?

STUART *(offended)* Alright, no need to be offensive!

MARCUS Why not? You have the nerve to play squash with my wife at the gym and she talks about you all the time. So why shouldn't I be as offensive as I like when it comes to her? I mean she spends more time with *you* than she does me.

STUART Really? Well did she go to the gym the last two weeks while I was on my holiday?

MARCUS She did actually. She told me that she met some guy named Stefano and played squash with him while you were away. He also plays with your wife I believe?

STUART Exactly! Did you know Stefano is Gay!? No, you didn't did you? And I will say this to you again - I am *married!* So for one Amanda is not doing anything with me. Secondly; I am happily *married* to Samantha and thirdly; I am definitely *'not gay'* as that tape says I am! I've got four kids for Christ's sake! That's from your brother who *you believe* is having an affair with your wife. Unbelievable!

MARCUS That's all well and good, but it doesn't prove anything, a lot of gay men get married to hide it from their families, why should you be any different?

STUART *(annoyed)* And you wonder why I haven't seen you in eight years! My god Marcus, you are still a bigoted old git aren't you?

MARCUS Am I? Well I am not the one who plays squash with my wife everyday other day am I? And I will believe you if you say that there is nothing going on between you – for now; but in all these years we haven't spoken you have never even visited Alexis have you?

STUART No, not much, that is true. But I do see a lot of her, more than you think actually.

MARCUS *(suspiciously)* What do you mean?

STUART You don't think I would come here to see her when you were home do you? I wait until you go away on your regular jollies, sorry, business trips. All the family comes, Samantha and the kids; we have a right old knees up.

MARCUS *(stunned)* Amanda never told me this. How many times have you visited?

STUART *(smug)* Ooh, I don't know. Probably thirty times over the years. Once this year, maybe eight times last year and that time when you had to go to Hong Kong for ten days we stayed over for a week. All of us slept in the attic bedroom. That was a great time. Then we went up to Edinburgh and saw some of the Festival. It was fantastic, marvellous.

MARCUS *(stunned)* Amanda tells me that she is bored out of her mind and shops all the time. Why would she keep this a secret from me?

STUART *(taunting)* Because it's *you* that's why.
MARCUS *(puzzled)* And what does that mean?
STUART I mean that you don't like anybody having any fun. Amanda tells me that you are "boring as hell" when you're home. You never go to the pub, or the cinema or even the garden centre on a Sunday. You don't do anything and you especially don't like spending any money. So why you have inherited fourteen mill is beyond me. It would just be put in forty offshore accounts earning interest while you drive around in that battered old Jaguar.
MARCUS *(proudly)* There is nothing wrong with that car! I bought it from new and it's never let me down.
STUART I don't know how, it's fifteen years old and it's second hand at that, not new.
MARCUS *(bridles)* Alright, it's not quite new, but only by six months, it was a demonstration car. It does its job. Why should I change it? Anyway, don't change the subject about you staying here while I'm on business trips and I am not 'boring as hell' as she says I am!
STUART Really? Okay, tell me something that you have done in, say, the last year, something that you, Amanda and Alexis did together that you really enjoyed as a family? Come on.
MARCUS *(thinks hard)* Ahh, what about the fireworks in the park? That was a really good evening, we had toffee apples, black peas, candy floss and rode the fairground rides. So there Poirot.
STUART Oh yes, I remember. That was a free event wasn't it? Oh no, it was a five pound entry and as many times as you wanted on the rides with free black peas to anyone who survived the 'haunted house'. Wow Marcus, you really pushed the boat out that night. A grand total of fifteen pounds you spent.
MARCUS *(proudly)* Nearer twenty five if you count toffee apples and candy floss.
STUART *(amazed)* You see, this is what I'm saying about you. Twenty five pounds doesn't even cover the cost of a bottle of wine at the restaurant that we all eat at.
MARCUS *(shocked)* What restaurant? When do you eat? Who with?
STUART *(smugly)* Macaroni's, the Italian in town. We all go, Amanda and Alexis too. It costs me a fortune, but it's a great evening.
MARCUS *(surprised)* But I eat there as well, it's my favourite restaurant.
STUART I know, the staff tell me that you don't even tip, even after you've frequented the place for six years. *(mocking)* And you don't even take your wife and daughter when you go. That's really mean don't you think? So I don't think you moaning about me playing squash with your wife can be put in the same context. Do you?
MARCUS Yes, but the difference is *I* am married to her, not you! What does Samantha think of all this squash playing?
STUART Samantha is perfectly fine with it, after all, they do go shopping together.
MARCUS Of course, I should have guessed. Well Stuart you have certainly opened my eyes this evening. Until now I wasn't aware of Amanda's secret life. It looks to me that I am indeed ostracised by my own family – with you of all people!
STUART You are the maker of your life Marcus. If you opened up your wallet more

and treated your wife and child to little gifts that show you appreciate them you may find them being less hostile towards you. One thing you could do is join the gym, you're looking very flabby round the middle. When was the last time you saw your feet?
MARCUS And the insults still come. Why would I want to join the gym?
STUART Well for one thing you would get fit, but the main thing is you will also see your wife a lot more. Or you will end up as a twenty five stone lonely miserable man in his eight bedroomed mansion with an empty photo album and a half eaten chicken from Sainsbury's for company. Do you still go to Sainsbury's before it closes and buy those reduced priced full chickens?
MARCUS Why are you mocking me?
STUART I'm making up for lost time, I've had eight years to think of loads of things.
MARCUS *(sadly)* You have also had eight years being a father to Alexis too. I will think about what you have just told me. No doubt there is more that I haven't been told and for the moment I do not wish to hear about it. The first thing I will do is have a chat with Amanda about what you have – well, shocked me with quite frankly.
STUART Well done, you're on the right track. Just don't be bolshy with her, be nice and friendly, she will be surprised that you are asking her, but probably glad that is all out in the open. You never know, she might let you back in bed with her *(winks)*
MARCUS *(ashen)* Is there anything about my marriage that you don't know?
STUART *(smiling)* I know more about you than you do, considering I haven't seen you for nearly eight years. Now come on, let's chat with this Frodsham guy about this stupid will.

They move to exit.

MARCUS His name is Forshaw. Albert Forshaw.
STUART Doesn't exactly roll off the tongue like "Bond, James Bond", does it?

Marcus looks blank.

Oh lighten up will you?

He slaps Marcus on the back. They exit.

<u>END OF SCENE THREE</u>

SCENE FOUR Two hours later.

Marcus, Amanda, Alexis, Forshaw and Stuart are discussing the will.

MARCUS *(puzzled)* Run that by me again Albert.
STUART *(annoyed)* Good grief, how many more times do we need to hear this? The solicitors have made an error, a mistake, a balls up! Whichever way you say it, it isn't good!
MARCUS That is easy for you to say, but how could Henry's will get 'lost'? Impossible!
ALBERT And as I have explained, a great many documents have been transferred onto the computer system and unfortunately it seems that your both uncle Henry's written will from nineteen eighty seven and the computer filed document have both disappeared.
MARCUS Well isn't that convenient? So this tape is the only proof that there is a will? It's just not good enough! I mean, you contacted me about it straight away as you had Henry's instructions to do so, surely that is a will isn't it?
ALBERT Not really sir, I had Henry's personal details, address, names of nearest relatives and only a hand written draft of his will. It isn't a legal will until it is on our stationary, signed and dated by the plaintiff and the solicitor.
MARCUS So why did you bother to tell me about his death and the will if you knew that it wasn't a 'legal document'? Why didn't you wait until the proper documentation was found?
ALBERT I thought it prudent that you should know sir.
MARCUS Really? So technically I shouldn't even have that box of tapes should I? Which means you have breached whatever the hell you shouldn't have done and I wouldn't have heard the tape that puts mine and my daughter's life in jeopardy!
ALBERT *(embarrassed)* Well you may have a point there sir.
MARCUS *(angrily)* I think I have more than a point Albert!
AMANDA Calm down Marcus. Obviously there has been an error on Albert's part. He is after all our solicitor as well as being Henry's solicitor and his loyalty to Henry has put him in the situation he finds himself in. Am I correct Albert.
ALBERT (*humbled*) Correct ma'am.
MARCUS Rubbish! There is more to this than fourteen million pounds you know! Albert may have broken the rules reading from an unsigned handwritten will but what I want to know why is – why?
ALBERT *(taken aback) Why* sir?
MARCUS Yes, why didn't you wait until the proper documentation was found? Why give me a box full of tapes? I find that strange in itself. Are you the one who is threatening me? Did you give me that box of tapes so that I would find the one with the threat?
ALBERT *(shocked)* No sir. It was a specific instruction by Henry before he died. He told me to give it to you personally as you love music.
MARCUS I do and it's obvious that he doesn't know me because I couldn't sit through that kind of music if my life depended on it!

STUART *(mocking)* Well it does doesn't it?
MARCUS *(turning on him)* Why don't you just shut up?!
ALBERT Sir, when I came here to inform you of your uncle Henry's passing I had the box with me. It was locked and I told you that it hadn't been opened for many years when I gave you the bunch of keys that came with it. I never knew of its contents, all I had was an envelope that had inside it a note to give it to you when he died. Which I did. It seems to me that I am just a scapegoat for this sorry mess.
MARCUS *(contrite)* I'm sorry Albert. Forgive me. You were very close to my uncle Henry towards the end. It just seems to me that you are part of a plot to kill me off or part of one of uncle Henry's practical jokes.
ALBERT If you had seen him in his final years you wouldn't say such a thing sir. He was very weak, every second was valuable to him. The last thing he was capable of was practical jokes.
MARCUS Well, not in the last few years of his life, but when he made that tape certainly.
ALBERT I didn't see your uncle all that often you know. I did arrange the nursing care that he received and a month or so before he died I had begun to make arrangements to put him in a nursing home, but he died the day before he was due to go.
STUART *(suspicious)* Why did you make these arrangements? What was uncle Henry to you?
ALBERT Well sir, he wasn't anything to me, but it seemed that his immediate family didn't care for him. You had long since stopped visiting him and it seemed so unfair for a once great man to be left to die so alone. I did my best for him, which is more than you two ever did and you were his last known family. So my motives, my interest in keeping him alive was far more rewarding to me than any of my other clients. But you two didn't see him, you never rang to find out about his welfare *(he pauses for effect, nobody takes him on, then angrily)* No, you didn't! All you are bothered about is what you will get from the will, which quite frankly in my opinion, you both shouldn't benefit from!

Marcus and Stuart are shamefaced, they know he's right, the mood becomes melancholic.

AMANDA Well, isn't this cheerful?
ALBERT That maybe so, but these two selfish people need to know how Henry suffered in his final years, but no; the money is the most important thing to them, all the rest is immaterial and it so annoys me!
AMANDA I know where you're coming from Albert, I really do. Marcus actually doesn't like spending money, so why his uncle Henry left so much to him is a complete mystery. Now Stuart on the other hand loves to spend money and isn't shy in giving people treats now and again, are you?
STUART *(proudly)* Money is for spending now, worry about the future when it happens is my motto.
MARCUS Well that is a stupid thing to say, you could be unemployed next week

and how will you be able to take my wife to Edinburgh when you have no money, eh?

AMANDA *(surprised)* How did you know about that? Have you two been talking?

STUART *(smug)* Oh yes, for the first time in eight years. It was most interesting I can tell you.

MARCUS Humiliating more like.

AMANDA Well you had to find out sometime. Though I must confess that I have been seriously tempted to tell you about Stuart many times. How does it feel that your brother is more of a father to your daughter than you will ever be? Not very good I should think.

MARCUS I don't think it's right that. . . .

AMANDA *(cutting in)* That what? If you were more of a man you would be here for us all the time instead of gallivanting around the world in whatever job it is that you do that is so secret you can't tell us! I'm fed up of being alone in this house. . . .

ALEXIS *(protesting)* Mum!

AMANDA You know what I mean dear, sorry; *we* are fed up of being alone in this house while you bugger off on business. At least Stuart and Samantha look after us and we always have a good time, don't we dear?

ALEXIS Yes mummy.

AMANDA I don't know what you are trying to achieve Marcus, but it is about time that you put your family first and forward and put whatever it is you do for your 'job' on the back-burner. Is it too much to ask for you to take us out for a meal or film once in a while? Or even the odd weekend break? Stop being such a tight-wad with your money and live a little. It's not asking for much is it?

MARCUS Well funnily enough I did want to talk to you about what you have been up to with Stuart over the years, but that can wait; but I did also want to say that I can understand him and his family being so good to you while I've been away and it's incredible that I never knew about it. Though I did wonder where some of the strange objects that appeared in the house came from and now I know why. But you must understand that my job could be terminated any time and all I am am doing is storing up a nest egg for the future and I get punished for it. Makes me wonder why I've bothered all these years.

AMANDA I'm not having a go at you, all I want is for you to give us some of your time every now and again. Is that too much to ask? And don't play the poor man with me – I know how much you are worth even before this inheritance, so don't kid a kidder kid because I'm not kidding.

MARCUS The only way you know how much I have is by going through my bank statements. But they were always sealed when I opened them, so how do you know?

AMANDA A kettle and Pritt stick. Easy really.

STUART You devious cow! I'm impressed!

AMANDA Touché! *(to Marcus)* You know, with the money you already have you could not only retire but keep us in holidays to the Caribbean for the next thirty years. I just don't understand why you are so tight fisted. Spending the odd bit of money on your family now and again won't hurt you you know.

MARCUS I know dear, but to put it quite simply, *(shame faced)* I don't know how to spend money.

AMANDA *(huffing)* You can say that again.

MARCUS *(embarrassed)* It's true! Apart from the two cars and this house, spending money is alien to me. My parents always told me to invest for the future, which this house is – and it's value has shot up nearly three hundred percent since we moved in, a considerable profit if I modestly say so. A fine investment don't you think?

AMANDA That is all well and good, but other than how much the house is worth you never invested in *us*, your wife and daughter. Surely we are more valuable to you than bricks and mortar?

MARCUS *(surprised)* Of course you are. You both are, isn't it obvious I think a lot of you?

AMANDA Well, that is a tricky question to answer. You believe you love us in your own weird way, Alexis and I think that you love your job more. If you do 'love' us, you will have to do a serious amount of persuading us that you do and the first thing that you can do is spend more time with us and not go swanning off around the world on those jollies that you never invite us to come along. Is that okay for now?

MARCUS Well I can't really give them up can I? It's my job. But maybe I can find out if you can both come along with me on some of them, how's that?

AMANDA Sounds good for starters.

MARCUS Though you may find that they are not as glamorous as you think they are. There is a lot of waiting around in conference halls, listening to boring speeches. . . .

AMANDA *(cutting in)* I am not holding your hand while you do your job you know! Alexis and I will go shopping or sightseeing, won't we dear.

ALEXIS Ooh, yes please mummy.

MARCUS *(angrily)* You see, this is why I won't take you with me. Already you are spending money and. . . .

AMANDA *(Interrupting)* Oh stop being such a Scrooge will you! On every trip abroad have you ever brought anything back for us? You know, a tacky souvenir, a trinket, anything? No, you haven't. And before you say what I know you are going to say – goody bags from conferences do not count as a gift!

MARCUS *(stunned)* Well I'm certainly learning a few things about myself tonight. I hadn't realised that you both saw me the way that you do. I will endeavour to be more generous with both my time, money and trips abroad in the future. Maybe if you both give me some gentle nudging I might not find it too bad spending, er, some money. It might be fun.

AMANDA *(amused)* There you go, that wasn't so hard was it?

STUART *(applauding)* Bravo old boy.

ALEXIS *(pleased)* Yes, well done daddy.

AMANDA And one of the first things that you can do is let me have another credit card with one hundred grand top limit.

MARCUS Hang on, you already have a credit card that needs paying off. How many do you need?

AMANDA I need as many as I need, one credit card is never enough.

ALEXIS And I want a horse. All my friends have horses and they laugh at me because they think we are poor. Can I have a horse daddy?

MARCUS (*surprised)* A horse? Aren't you too old for a horse now? Shouldn't you have wanted a horse when you're eight or something? Wouldn't a car be better?

ALEXIS Pleeeaassseee? I don't care if I'm twenty eight, I want one!

MARCUS Whoa, whoa! Hold on here, don't let's get carried away, let me spend my money gradually, otherwise you two would make me bankrupt within a month!

STUART *(heartily)* Welcome to my world Marcus! I live off my overdraft, if the bank stopped it I would be well screwed I can tell you!

MARCUS *(to Amanda)* You see dear, this is why I am so careful with my money. You only have to look at Stuart here to see what overspending beyond your means can do to a bank account. I am not saying that I won't treat you to what you want, but in moderation only. That is my only condition, is that fair?

AMANDA *(resigned)* Fair enough. But I do want a credit card.

MARCUS *(snapping)* Yes, yes, yes! You can have one, but with an upper limit of fifty thousand alright?

AMANDA *(smugly)* Certainly. Thank you.

She kisses his cheek, then whispers in his ear, giggling, Marcus goes red.

ALEXIS What about my horse daddy?

MARCUS Well, I won't buy you a horse because you quickly get tired of things, but what I will do is let you join the riding school in the village and we'll take it from there, how's that?

ALEXIS *(pleased, hugs him)* Brill! Thanks daddy!

MARCUS I will only do this for you if you stop calling me "daddy", as you constantly like to remind me, you are seventeen going on eighteen, it's about time you grew out of it. Deal?

ALEXIS Yes. "Daddy". *(hugs him again)*

MARCUS *(huffing)* It's a bloody good job I have come into money, you two will bleed me dry I know it!

ALBERT Well sir, you haven't yet and your brother contests the will, so until the correct paperwork can be found the will will be held in trust until it can be released.

MARCUS *(annoyed)* Oh bloody hell! Did you have to remind me Albert?!

ALBERT *(sheepish)* Sorry sir.

Marcus goes to the drinks cabinet and pours himself a drink as Amanda and Stuart try to stifle giggles.

END OF ACT ONE

ACT TWO Two evenings later.

Turner and Glover have arrived. Marcus is impatiently pacing the room.

MARCUS *(impatiently)* Well, it looks like you two have a reprieve regarding this cassette business regarding my daughters and my life. Your immediate superior has verified that you two are police officers, I am sure you understand that a person of my high standing has to take all the necessary precautions, especially due to the nature of the circumstances.
TURNER And quite right if I may so Mr Winstanley, caution is prudent.
MARCUS Yes, well, it was lucky for you both that your C.O. holds you in such regard, despite your track records. So, what is this new piece of 'evidence' that you couldn't tell me over the phone?
TURNER Well sir, it is concerning the tape, our lab boys have analysed it and it is a tape from around the mid nineteen eighties, so from that angle of the case it is authentic.
MARCUS *(triumphant)* Yes! I knew it! So it could be used as a last will and testament then?
TURNER No sir.
MARCUS Why not?
GLOVER The recording isn't a genuine one sir.
MARCUS *(surprised)* What do you mean? If it's a genuine tape then the recording is genuine, it has to be.
GLOVER It is a recording that has been placed over the top of a previous one sir.
MARCUS *(puzzled)* What do you mean?
TURNER The recording on the tape was recorded over another recording. The lab boys haven't managed to separate the two recordings yet, but they are slowly getting there.
MARCUS Well I wish they would hurry up, I've only got two days left to live!
TURNER I realise that sir, but it's something that cannot be rushed.
MARCUS *(angry)* Fine, take your time and then you will be playing the recording to my grieving wife and child!
TURNER No need for that tone sir, we are doing our best.
MARCUS Yes of course you are. I'm sorry, it's just nerve racking for me that's all.
GLOVER We understand.
MARCUS So the recording on the tape is a recording on top of another is it? How did the lab boys find that out? Surely if the original has been recorded over with something else then it has gone for good hasn't it?
TURNER Not necessarily sir. You see, the new recording has simply layered itself over the "original recording" shall we call it. What must have happened is the "erase head" did not "erase" the original recording. It only came to light because you listened to the recording on a one track playback system. The original recording had simply not been recorded over; it was still there, unheard by your one track cassette

player.
MARCUS *(puzzled)* Sorry for being dense, but you are talking in riddles.
TURNER I am explaining this as simply as I can. It seems that the cassette recorder used to record the voice of your dead uncle had not completely recorded over the previous recording and therefore it is still layered "underneath" what you have heard; I.E. the death threat. The lab boys are trying to separate the two recordings, which I might also add had been picked up by very very sophisticated equipment usually used for surveillance purposes. *(proudly)* Many of them my cases.
MARCUS *(putting her down)* Which you told me you never solved. That gives me great confidence I must say! And do the lab boys know what the recording is that had been rerecorded over?
GLOVER *(bristling)* Well as yet they can't be certain, but it could be a spoken voice.
MARCUS Really? Not music like all the other tapes?
GLOVER No sir, the wavelength patterns are different compared to music patterns.
MARCUS So it could be uncle Henry dictating a different draft of the will?
TURNER Until the two recordings are separated it would be too early to speculate on that matter sir.
MARCUS Well I am going to speculate that it is and it would most probably prove that the tape we've heard is probably a fake all along.
GLOVER Or it could be real. I wouldn't relax too much with the death threat hanging over you sir.
MARCUS *(sarcastic)* Aren't you a bundle of joy Constable Glover.
GLOVER No need to take that tone sir, I merely stated that. . . .
MARCUS *(interrupting, impatiently)* Yes yes, I know, I know.
GLOVER We would appreciate it if you kept this information to just us sir. If any of your family made the recording that you say is your uncle Henry it could compromise our investigation.
MARCUS Certainly, as you wish, but the general feeling within the family is that it is a fake anyway.
TURNER Have you replayed the copy we made for you? Was it helpful?
MARCUS Yes I have. To my brother Stuart the other night.
TURNER And what does he think about it?
MARCUS Well he thinks that the voice of uncle Henry is genuine.
TURNER *(surprised)* Really?
MARCUS Yes. You see he visited uncle Henry far more often than I did, though not very many times in his last few years. He recognised Henry's voice straight away.
TURNER I see. And what was his reaction when he heard all the money was to go to you?
MARCUS Well, he was outraged, what would you think his reaction would be?
TURNER Understandable. On our first visit you told us that you hadn't seen your brother in eight years.
MARCUS Yes, well, unfortunately I had to speak to him because of this will nonsense. He was certainly angry when he discovered all Henry's money was to be left to me I can tell you.
TURNER Of course. So are you talking to each other now? Eight years is a long

time isn't it?

MARCUS It is, but I am not the one who stopped the talking. We were quite close once.

TURNER *(stunned)* Really? Explain sir.

MARCUS *(reluctant)* Do I have to? It's not that exciting I can assure you.

TURNER Let me the judge of that Misterr Winstanley.

MARCUS *(pouring himself a drink. Finally)* Well, if you insist. It goes back a long time, since school in fact. Stuart and I have always been competitive, even though we are chalk and cheese. We both worked for the Government as advisers to Number Ten. Anyway, eight years ago a Ministerial post came up in the Home Office that we were both equally qualified for. It got to the stage in which we were the last two candidates – although I didn't know about this until I got the post. At the time, it was deemed prudent that each candidate was unaware of the "competition" as it were. All sorts of documents had to be signed in the name of "National Security" and "Data Protection". Anyway, I got the position and I took us all out for a huge celebration meal, his family, my family and as it was also his birthday I thought we could celebrate the two together. But when I announced that I had got the post he stormed out of the restaurant claiming that I had 'stabbed him in the back' and that I was 'rubbing his nose in it on his birthday too'. Well I was shocked, I never knew – genuinely I did not know. He vowed never to speak to me again and up to two nights ago he didn't. For eight years.

GLOVER *(surprised)* He didn't speak to you for eight years because you got the job that he wanted? Would you have done the same to him sir?

MARCUS *(surprised)* No, definitely not. I would have been pleased for him. But he took it as a 'betrayal' and that's how it's been for all this time. The daft thing about it is that he kept his word and didn't speak to me, but he never stopped seeing Amanda and Alexis in all these years, as a sort of – I don't know what you would call it? "Mocking" I suppose.

TURNER *(puzzled)* Sorry sir, run that by me again. He didn't speak to you, but he continued to visit your wife and daughter?

MARCUS Correct. I'll make a police officer out of you yet.

TURNER *(stunned)* I am astonished.

MARCUS *(angrily) That* is an understatement! When I found out it took me all my strength not to knock his teeth out! Especially when I find that when I've been on business trips he and his family have been staying here or going up to Edinburgh to see the festival. It's like my wife and daughter have two different lives.

TURNER Indeed. Well, this is most interesting. We would like to have a chat with your brother as soon as we can. Have you any idea of his whereabouts?

MARCUS Yes, he's playing squash with my wife, they'll be here in ten minutes or so.

TURNER Excellent. Do you mind if we wait for him?

MARCUS Not at all, be my guest, I could do with the company now my daughter has gone to be weighed up for a horse.

TURNER *(taken aback)* Pardon sir.

MARCUS Oh sorry, talking aloud. My daughter has just joined a riding school, she's being given a choice of horses to ride depending on her weight and the horse's temperament with her. She's very excited about it.

GLOVER Young girls are sir, my daughter is just the same when it comes to horses, she loves them.

MARCUS *(surprised)* You have a daughter Detective Glover?

GLOVER *(proudly)* Three actually, seventeen, eleven and eight *(produces a wallet and shows Marcus a photo)* Hilary, Joanne and Petra. Lovely girls. Hilary was named after me.

MARCUS *(quietly amused)* I see, so your name is Hilary Glover is it? I like how you carry a photo of them in your wallet.

GLOVER *(surprised)* Why surprised sir? Don't you have a photo of your daughter in yours?

MARCUS *(shocked)* No, I have money and credit cards in mine. It's a wallet, it's what it's for.

TURNER *(with authority)* Glover, this isn't the time to be letting standards slip.

GLOVER *(meekly)* Sorry ma'am.

TURNER Quite alright Glover, but when we are on duty we do not fraternise, is that clear?

GLOVER *(embarrassed)* Perfectly.

MARCUS *(breaking the tension)* Would you both like a cup of tea?

TURNER Yes please. Glover?

GLOVER Same for me too.

MARCUS Fine, I'll go and make a pot, won't be a tick *(exits)*

Turner goes to the door and waits for a moment to make sure that Marcus isn't listening.

TURNER Well Glover, apart from a moment of sentiment on your part; what do you think of our Marcus Winstanley?

GLOVER I think he is genuine and is just as bemused at the tape as we are.

TURNER And his family?

GLOVER Well ma'am, that I am not able to figure out. The wife doesn't seem all that concerned about her husband's possible death threat and neither does the daughter considering her life is in danger too.

TURNER So what do you conclude on what you have observed so far?

GLOVER Well ma'am, I think that his wife and child made that recording.

TURNER That is my thinking too. For one the daughter didn't look all that concerned at the news of her possible demise. In fact, she is very upbeat about it. Very strange in my book, don't you think Glover?

GLOVER Well ma'am, she is seventeen and her mind is obviously on other things. She most likely doesn't take the threat seriously.

TURNER *(agreeing)* Exactly my thinking Glover! Marcus Winstanley has been so shaken up by the threat he hasn't returned to his job, he has taken 'overdue leave' and has the daughter been withdrawn from college? No. She insists on going, regardless of the threat. And that is something I cannot figure out Glover. Why? If that was me I

would lock myself in my bedroom and never venture out; but not our Alexis, her routine is no different.
GLOVER Well ma'am, that's kids for you. They don't see the danger until a split second before it happens. I should know having three girls who are more interested in texting and going on Facebook twenty four seven. A mother knows these things.
TURNER Maybe *you* do being a parent. I am not a parent, so I don't know what kids are like. Keep your eyes on the daughter and let me know of anything you think is suspicious, no matter how trivial. Understand?
GLOVER Perfectly ma'am.
TURNER Good. I will finally have a solved case at last and I won't get demoted. Finally; something good will happen to me and that is great news don't you think?
GLOVER Yes ma'am.
TURNER *(proudly)* There is no way I'm going back in uniform. In fact, this case could be the making of me.
GLOVER *(shocked)* And me.
TURNER *(narked)* Yes of course, you would want to share the glory as well. Well when we do, the first ten rounds are on you. How does that sound?
GLOVER *(unsure)* Er. . . . .

Marcus enters carrying a tray of tea items and biscuits.

TURNER Tell me later. Ahh, tea *and* biscuits as well. Well Mister Winstanley, you are spoiling us!
MARCUS *(proudly)* Nothing but the best for you two. The biscuits are Foxes creams, my favourites. I hide them from Alexis as she would eat the whole packet if she found them. There's two each for you. Would you like me to be mum?

They nod, Marcus pours out three teas. Turner and Glover busy themselves adding sugar etc.

I'll leave the sugars to yourselves. So how do you think this case is going? Would it be cracked by the deadline day?
TURNER Well I hope so sir. We'll know more once the sounds off the tape have been separated and analysed, but Glover and I have a very strong idea about who is responsible for the tape. But unfortunately we cannot divulge that information to you just yet.
MARCUS Off course you can't, "Data Protection" and all that crap! But don't worry, I have my own theory of who made that tape.
TURNER *(surprised)* Really? Who?
MARCUS My wife. *(no response)* Well it's obvious isn't it?
TURNER *(shocked)* What makes you say that sir?
MARCUS Isn't it obvious? *(no response)* Okay I'll tell you. She hates me, she hates my job and the fact that I am always away on Government business and when I am not on business all I do is vegetate in front of the telly. And also I don't take them anywhere or spend any money on them – perfect reason, perfect suspect I reckon.

GLOVER *(shocked)* That is a bit harsh sir.
MARCUS You won't be saying that when she's handcuffed in the back of a police van, oh no! Just watch her and see if there is any flicker of worry for me. I bet you don't see any. Oh, I can see by your faces that you both think the same way as me. So, when does she get arrested for plotting to kill me?
TURNER Well she isn't a 'suspect' as you so delicately put it, but who is to say that *you* could also be a suspect?
MARCUS *(surprised)* Me? How ridiculous!
TURNER Well if you don't mind me saying so everyone can be a suspect. There is a lot of money involved, so we cannot rule anybody out.
MARCUS *(amazed)* Have you any idea how ridiculous that sounds? How can you have 'suspects' when the main protagonist is dead? Next thing you'll be telling me is that you suspect my daughter! Are you two for real?
TURNER Sir, we have to look at every angle we can to determine probable cause from everybody involved in the investigation. No stone will be left unturned to ensure you and your daughters safety. You can be certain of that fact.
MARCUS Well, fancy words if you don't mind me saying so. But let's see what happens on the night of our 'death', which I hope you will be around to witness.
GLOVER Oh don't worry sir, we won't miss your death, just by the simple fact you might have proved us wrong. In fact I would go as far as saying. . . .
TURNER *(angrily cutting in)* Shut up Glover!
GLOVER *(meekly)* Yes ma'am.
MARCUS No, I would like to hear what she has to say. Do you have an idea as to who it could be who's threatening me?
GLOVER Sorry sir, I cannot say, "confidentiality" and all that.
MARCUS Typical of the police force today! No back bone. Too busy giving speeding tickets to innocent law breaking motorists than investigating a 'real case'. Well you'll be sorry when I've been murdered by uncle Henry's assassinater, just you see. And then you'll be demoted anyway! I don't think you two are taking my death threat seriously.
TURNER *(a slur on her duty)* I can assure you that we are doing our utmost to ensure your safety on the day sir.
MARCUS *(sarcastic)* Great, that's all I can ask for then isn't it?
TURNER *(annoyed)* It seems to me sir that *you* are not taking the threat towards your life seriously.
MARCUS *(surprised)* Really? Well I can assure you that I am, but what you rather me do? Cry my heart out or just shrug it off as an 'oh well'? I cannot be the master of my destiny, it is in the hands of another party and until I know I am in the clear – then I will party! Ooh, I've just made a little joke there.
TURNER *(deadpan)* Really sir, I didn't spot it.
MARCUS Never mind. You plods weren't trained to have a sense of humour were you?
GLOVER Not on a murder case sir no.
MARCUS *(shocked)* Why say that? It isn't a murder case until I've been murdered and I haven't been murdered yet have I? *(outraged)* Bloody hell, you're both keen to

see me bumped off aren't you?!
TURNER *(mocking)* Not really sir, but we do have other cases to solve you know.
MARCUS You make me sound like a Rubik's Cube!
TURNER I apologise if that's how you feel sir.
MARCUS Oh don't be, I could never figure them out, just as I couldn't figure out those magic eyes. Freaky!
TURNER You say that your brother wasn't very happy when he found out that you had inherited your uncles entire estate. Did he show any signs of knowing that a threat had been made towards you at all?
MARCUS I don't understand the question.
TURNER Did your brother show any surprise when he was told that your life was in danger or did he 'shrug' it off as your imaginative imagination?
MARCUS Well as far as I noticed he was shocked. *(thinks)* Yes, his reaction was one of pure shock. Why do you ask? Do you think that he made the taped recording?
TURNER As I told you earlier sir, I wouldn't like to speculate, but he could also be a possible suspect.
MARCUS *(surprised)* I don't see how. He was very annoyed when he heard that Henry's entire estate was to be left to me. And unless he's taken acting lessons, he was very convincing.
TURNER I am not doubting for one moment the relationship you and your brother have, but we need to establish a motive. When your brother discovered your life had been threatened did he show any remorse?
MARCUS As I said; unless he's been taking acting lessons he was very convincing. So you suspect him also?
TURNER We cannot rule anybody out sir, not even you as I have just said.
MARCUS *(surprised)* Don't be daft! I am the one that's been threatened.
GLOVER And your daughter don't forget.
MARCUS *(annoyed)* Yes I *know!* Now why would I want to threaten my own life? Go on, please explain as I am extremely intrigued!
TURNER Well sir, you say that you were the first to hear the tape, what is to say that you didn't make the tape recording to throw us of the scent.
MARCUS *(incredulous)* Are you *saying* that you think that *I* made the tape? For what reason would I benefit when I have already inherited fourteen million quid? I think you are just grasping at straws now. No wonder your C.O. wants to demote you.
TURNER That is a little harsh sir. You may have your opinion on whether we can do our job or whether we cannot, but our number one priority is you and your daughters welfare and as I have told you previously; no harm will come to either of you.
MARCUS Yes of course, forgive me – again, for my outburst. It is something that is hard to get to grips with, you know, a threat against your life? It kind of makes me wish that I had done a lot more with it and lived a little. Stuart lives by the day, he couldn't give a monkeys about tomorrow until tomorrow arrives and then it's just 'another day'. But that's him, it's the way he is and I am the way I am. I feel rather pathetic compared to him.
TURNER No sir, I wouldn't say that.
MARCUS Oh I do! Come off it! Wait till you meet him and then decide who you

would rather go to the pub with when the case is solved. I mean, my wife has had enough of me, my daughter thinks this is all one big joke. It's like everybody is conspiring against me and it's getting me down I can tell you.
He has suddenly become melancholic. Turner indicates to Glover that they should go, they move to the door.

TURNER Well sir, we'd better be getting back to the station. Thank you for the cuppa.

Marcus doesn't look up, he is sobbing.

(embarrassed) Okay, we'll see you in two days' time. Er, bye.

She quickly ushers Glover out of the room and they exit.

END OF SCENE ONE

ACT TWO: SCENE TWO The 'threat' night.

Everybody bar Turner and Glover are gathered in the lounge. The mood is tense.

MARCUS *(to Albert)* I don't understand how the written transcript of the will has been lost. I'm sure you had it with you when you came here with the tapes? Are you sure you haven't mislaid it somewhere?
ALBERT Positive sir. And I never said I had a written transcript. I merely stated that there was one that documented what your uncle said on the tape. But unfortunately I cannot find it on either the manual records or on the computer system.
MARCUS It all seem very convenient doesn't it? Anyway, the police have come up with something very interesting that I have deliberately kept from you all and they will be here any time now to confirm what I know; that you don't know.
ALBERT *(surprised)* Oh? And what would that be?
MARCUS *(refraining from being smug)* Well, the police have told me that the recording that we have all heard is not an *original* recording. It could possibly be a 'rerecording' that has been placed over what could be uncle Henry's original recording of his last will and testament.
STUART *(shocked)* Hang on, what are you saying? Do the police think that uncle Henry made that recording on top of another? I don't understand what you are going on about. It is his voice, I'm certain of it.
MARCUS *(grandly)* Oh I have no doubt that it is uncle Henry's voice on that tape, but the police took the original away for examination and they have told me that under the recording of what we 'think' is uncle Henry's voice, there is another recording that didn't get completely 'wiped' I think the term is.
ALEXIS *(tensing)* And what have they said it could be daddy?
MARCUS Well they are one hundred percent certain it is a spoken voice.
STUART What do you mean – a 'spoken voice'?

MARCUS Apparently the waveforms differ from a spoken voice to that of music and it transpires that the original recording wasn't completely erased by the "new" recording So D.I. Turner has got the lab boys working overnight to separate the two recordings and any minute now she will be here with them and all this will business can finally be sorted as to who gets what. Interesting don't you think?
STUART Well not for you if it turns out that the original recording hasn't left you with fourteen million, you'll look quite a chump won't you?
MARCUS Maybe I will, but if it proves that the recording that we've heard is for some reason false, then my daughter and I have no reason to be scared by a so called 'death threat'. And to me, that is the most important thing, and if I look a 'chump'; then so what?

He hugs Alexis. Stuart becomes tense and moves to the window, as he does so he briefly squeezes Amanda's shoulder which doesn't go unnoticed by Marcus.

ALBERT It doesn't change anything sir. As I have explained to you many times, the will is only valid when it is on our stationary and signed by the plaintiff and executor. That is the law I'm afraid.
MARCUS Really? Well if it is the 'law', why did you give me the box of cassettes in the first place? Was it written in Henry's will that I should receive those tapes or have you bent the rules because you, *you* wanted me to find that tape and you are secretly laughing at me? Hmm? Come on, admit it, you of all people know what is legal and what isn't and somehow my daughter and I have been put in a position that jeopardises us both. And what of this Michael Stevens who died five years ago? He isn't on any of your letter heads, so my suspicious mind thinks 'strange, not to worry though, Henry knows best'. This whole will business has stressed me out the last two weeks and quite frankly it is annoying me.
STUART *(cheerfully)* Well if you feel that way about it, then I will gladly have the money if it comes to me.
MARCUS And you are welcome to it. It has caused me nothing but misery the last two weeks and if that is what such an amount of money does to people then quite frankly you can keep it.
AMANDA *(shocked)* Marcus!
MARCUS Oh come off it Amanda, you never showed any worry or panicked when you heard the tape and that death threat made towards me. And you didn't really seem all that concerned when the date of my being 'bumped off' was on that written transcript. Have you an ulterior motive? (*He lets the question hang)*
AMANDA *(angrily, realises what he has said)* Are you saying that you *think* I am the one who made that tape? Why would I do that?
MARCUS I can think of fourteen million reasons, but maybe I am just being "paranoid".
AMANDA *(angrily)* I think you definitely are being paranoid. I heard that tape the same time that you did and I was just as shocked as you were! Whatever is going on in that head of yours just stop it – now! I do love you, even though you are tighter than a ducks arse, but there is no way I would wish you dead, I mean, why would I?

MARCUS *(sarcastic)* Why would you indeed? Well, until the police arrive with their evidence I am suspecting everybody in this room.
ALEXIS (*stunned*) Even me daddy? But my life has been threatened too.
MARCUS Well not you obviously. Sorry, I worded that wrong. You all know what I mean. We all have suspicions that the tape is not what it seem to be and see it from my point of view. Why would my uncle Henry leave me such a huge amount of money then want to bump me off? Albert suddenly loses the original documentation, my wife shows no interest in my ominous demise and my daughter carries on as if nothing is going to happen to her. Stuart is understandably annoyed about being squeezed out from the will and naturally contests it. And the police suspect everybody, including me. They say that uncle Henry could have been forced to make that recording, me I am not too sure about it as I was when I first heard it and I cannot decide if it is real or a fake. But whatever the outcome I am taking the threat on mine and Alexis's possible demise seriously.
AMANDA *(whispering to Albert)* This is your fault you know.
ALBERT *(shocked)* Me? How do you work that out ma'am?
AMANDA Well, losing the written transcript for one. How could you be so careless?
ALBERT Well ma'am, blame the demands of modern technology, not me. I am simply the deliverer of the will. I will not be executor until it is proved to be true and accurate.
AMANDA *(disbelieving)* Yeah right. You change your mind as often as you change your socks! Why should I believe you now?
ALBERT Well for one, I do not wear socks ma'am.
AMANDA (*surprised)* Pardon?
ALBERT Never mind.
MARCUS Look, forget socks will you please? It is near to the time I am going to get bumped off, show some compassion will you?
ALBERT Sorry sir.
AMANDA *(contrite)* Yes, sorry darling.
MARCUS Thank you. I wouldn't want the last thing I ever heard being the fact that Albert doesn't wear socks, it would be quite literally putting the boot in.

Amanda giggles.

(rounding on her) And what is so funny?
AMANDA You talking about socks and boots!
MARCUS *(confused)* And what is so funny about that?
AMANDA Think about it!
MARCUS I am and I still don't know what is so funny.
AMANDA *(to herself)* And people wonder why I am still with you.
MARCUS I heard that!
AMANDA *(sheepishly)* Sorry.
MARCUS Never mind. Anyway Albert, I have been doing some research and as far as I can tell, it doesn't matter if uncle Henry wrote his will on a beer mat – the recording we have all heard *is* a valid will. The only time it isn't 'valid' is if the

deceased hadn't made one, which would mean that everything the deceased had would go to the nearest relative, but the fact of uncle Henry's taped recording does make it valid. Therefore the will goes to me and all its contents. You know, the internet is a wonderful invention, so much information on it, I'm amazed at its simplicity too.

AMANDA *(stunned)* So the will is valid?

MARCUS Yes. I'm afraid Albert here has been stringing us along. A will can be recorded on anything, even on a beer mat, as I have just said.

AMANDA *(shocked)* Albert, how could you do such a thing to us?

ALBERT *(shocked)* Me? I cannot see how I am suddenly responsible for your husband's ignorance, all I am is the 'postman' so to speak. I have delivered the items – the tapes – and I am not responsible for their content. And since we heard the tape all we have done is discuss whether or not it is a fake, or who of us – if it is indeed any of us – made the tape. I refuse to be a made a scapegoat in all this and as of now I am terminating my involvement and my business with you and your family.

MARCUS In English please.

ALBERT I resign.

MARCUS I see. Well you will have to tell the police that you have 'resigned' because they want to talk to you about your sudden disappearance last week.

ALBERT And as I have explained to you I had some leave that I had to take.

MARCUS In the middle of a police investigation? The police think that is a rather peculiar thing to do. But then, what do I know about the matters of the law?

ALBERT I see. So because I had some leave and chose to take it in the last ten days it is suddenly peculiar?

MARCUS Well, more suspicious actually. But don't bother to tell us, save your tale for when the police arrive.

ALBERT *(offended)* I certainly will, and you will look such a fool when it is proved that I am innocent.

MARCUS Oh don't be so offended Albert, we are all suspects, nobody is innocent.

The doorbell rings.

(grandly) And here they are. I'm looking forward to hearing what the police have to tell us, should be interesting don't you think?

STUART More than interesting, I would say embarrassing, not to say humiliating if you don't get a penny from the will.

MARCUS I would say that my life and that of my daughter is worth more than fourteen million pounds wouldn't you think?

AMANDA *(sarcastic)* Not to me it isn't.

MARCUS Well you would say that wouldn't you? (*The doorbell sounds again).*

ALEXIS Shall I go daddy?

MARCUS Certainly.

She skips out of the room, everybody is uncomfortable and avoids looking at each other. A very serious looking Turner and Glover enter, Marcus worries, Amanda smiles at the possible good news.

TURNER Good evening everybody *(fixes her gaze on Albert)* and a good evening to the elusive Albert Forshaw. You have been very hard to trace the last few days. Any particular reason?
ALBERT *(uncomfortable)* I had some leave that was due to me.
TURNER *(suspiciously)* Really? Well you can explain later if you don't mind, this 'death threat' business needs to be resolved first.
MARCUS *(impatiently)* Yes, hurry up and give me the bad news.
TURNER *(opening up a small cassette box)* Of course sir, no need to panic.
MARCUS *(panicking)* No need to panic? Is it your life that is danger? No, it's mine. So let's get this out of the way shall we?
TURNER Well I have a lot of good news to tell you mister Winstanley, first of all I have to inform you that your life and indeed the life of your daughter is perfectly safe. You are in no danger and this 'death threat' from nineteen eighty seven is indeed – a fake.

Marcus is overcome with relief and he and Alexis hug each other jubilantly.

However.
MARCUS *(breaking off, stunned)* However? What do you mean 'however'? 'However' what?
TURNER As our suspicions confirmed now that we have separated the two sound recordings we do believe that it is indeed a fake recording that you heard and I will tell you more later. But first I must play you the original recording. Glover.

Glover puts a tape into a player and presses play. The voice of Henry is heard.

HENRY *(on tape)* Is this on? *(cough)* My name is Henry Goodfellow and this is a recording of my last will and testament that is also being written down by my solicitor Michael Stevens. As I have no immediate family that I can leave my money and effects too I therefore bequeath everything to my family solicitor Michael Stevens and his family.
STEVENS *(on tape, stunned)* Pardon? Are you sure sir?
HENRY *(on tape)* Of course I'm bloody sure! Now get writing will you!

Glover stops the tape.

MARCUS *(stunned)* What?! I don't understand, how?
GLOVER *(to Stuart)* Would you confirm that is the voice of your uncle?
STUART I would say that is is yes. I think so, it sounds like him.
MARCUS *(puzzled)* Hang on, are you saying that I don't receive anything at all?
TURNER No sir, not on the evidence on the recording. Play the rest of the tape Glover.

Glover resumes the tape.

HENRY *(on tape)* I do not make this decision lightly. But my brother, who I longed since disowned will *not receive* a penny as he does not deserve to inherit any of my wealth after the way he treated his wife for the last eight years. Divorcing him was the best thing she could ever have done. Actually Michael, I'll leave her a million, which should be adequate compensation for her husband having two bastard children with that floozy. And that is my final say in how my money and properties will be divided. If I should live many more years I may possibly renew my will *if* I change my mind. Now read back to me what I have just said, get it typed up tomorrow and I will sign it.

Glover stops the tape. There is a slow realisation of what has just been said.

MARCUS *(stunned)* Is that it? Is there any more?
GLOVER No sir, the recording ended there.
MARCUS *(crestfallen)* So I don't get a penny?
AMANDA *(sarcastic)* Oh dear and you had *so* many plans to spend that money. Oh well, we'll just have to live in poverty for the rest of our lives.
MARCUS *(nastily)* Oh shut up Amanda! There is no need to be like that!
AMANDA *(taken aback)* Sorry.
MARCUS *(angrily)* And so you should be! You mock me being such a spendthrift, but if you had inherited it it would have been gone in a year. And we aren't that badly off you know! *(to Turner)* So where do we go from here?
TURNER Well, now we have established that your uncle Henry has left you with nothing and his will wasn't renewed and that there is no death threat to you and your daughter, then technically police involvement has ceased. But there is the matter of the 'forged' recording that you heard and there is something that the lab boys discovered on the recording that technically makes the tape blackmail.
MARCUS I'm sorry for being a little dense here, but your case has gone from a 'death threat' to 'blackmail'? How?
TURNER Play the other tape Glover.

Glover complies. The voice of the 'fake' Henry is once again heard.

TURNER *(to Stuart)* Does that sound like your uncle Henry sir?
STUART Well now that I have heard each recording back to back I have to say that I am not sure.
TURNER Interesting. *(to Marcus)* And you sir, now you have heard the two recordings, would you also say that it sounds like your uncle?
MARCUS Well now I have heard them together I have to concur with Stuart and say that I am not sure.
STUART *(puzzled)* So what does this mean? Is that somebody impersonating Henry? Is that what you are getting at?
TURNER Yes.

STUART Well it is a very good one if I say so myself.
TURNER Yes it is. *(suddenly)* Mister Albert Forshaw I am arresting you on a charge of malicious intent and endangerment towards mister Marcus Winstanley and his daughter Alexis Winstanley. You do not have to say anything, but it may harm your defence if you do not say something that you may later rely on in court. Glover, the cuffs.

Glover moves to Albert and attempts to put the cuffs on, he moves out of the way and hinders her, it looks like a strange aerobics exercise. Everybody is shocked at what they have just heard.

GLOVER) Sir, will you put your hands down please?
ALBERT) I have never heard anything so ridiculous in all my life!
MARCUS *(amazed)* Albert?! But how? What evidence do you have?
TURNER *(to Glover)* Give it up Glover! We'll deal with him later.
GLOVER *(ceasing)* As you wish ma'am.
MARCUS Come on, explain yourselves.
TURNER If you insist. Mister Forshaw, please sit down. And you cannot leave this house as there are two policemen outside who have orders to arrest you on sight. Understand?
ALBERT *(sitting down)* Do I have a choice?
TURNER No.
ALBERT *(resigned)* Very well.
STUART *(impressed)* So it was you all along! Albert you old crafty dog! It takes some balls trying to get money out of my brother I can tell you! I would high five you if Glover would move out of the way.
MARCUS *(shocked)* Stuart!
TURNER *(with authority)* Yes sir, would you mind refraining from saying anything else or you will be on a charge of enticement.
STUART *(meekly)* Sorry.
MARCUS *(in disbelief)* I am shocked, amazed and saddened at you Albert! How could you do such a thing to us?
ALBERT *(protesting)* Sir, I had nothing to do with that recording on your life.
MARCUS *(scoffing)* Really? It was you who brought me that box of tapes and you had been quite close to my uncle Henry and these two certainly think you had some involvement against me, so there is no point in trying to wriggle your way out of it now is there?
TURNER Excuse me sir, let me do the questioning if you don't mind.
MARCUS *(surprised)* Oh, of course, certainly, go ahead. You are after all police officers and I am not.
TURNER That would be the best way sir, just listen and learn the ways of the force.
STUART *(to Amanda)* And you will be a Jedi knight!

They both giggle, Turner rounds on them.

TURNER And what is so funny?
STUART *(giggling)* Nothing. . . . Obi Wan!
TURNER *(skilfully ignores him)* Our investigations have come up with a very interesting fact regarding mister Forshaw and it will be a shock to you all; you see, mister Forshaw here is the *son* of mister Michael Stevens.

Murmurs of surprise.

And if you will let me explain please.
ALBERT *(resigned)* So you found out. I suppose it was inevitable in the end.
MARCUS But, I don't understand. How did you keep that fact from us?
TURNER He had motive sir. Being the son of Michael Stevens embarrassed Albert because Michael Stevens was a homosexual who had been cautioned by the police on numerous occasions for being a "practising homosexual", due to his what we would term now as 'cottaging'. But fortunately for him all charges were dropped because those involved either dropped the accusations or didn't turn up to court. He kept his life so secret he maintained his position of trust with the company of solicitor's he worked for. He had been having a relationship with your uncle for many years.
STUART *(amazed)* Uncle Henry a raving poofter eh? Who'd have thought it?
TURNER *(sternly)* Sir, I did ask you to be quiet. Please do not speak until you are asked to, is that clear?
STUART *(embarrassed)* Yes, of course. Sorry again.
TURNER Thank you. Now we know why mister Forshaw had disappeared for a few days and that was because last week was the anniversary of his father's death and you had to have time away to 'mourn' shall we say.
ALBERT *(quietly)* That is correct.
TURNER I apologise to you all and especially to you Mister Forshaw, if these facts cause you any distress, but Albert Forshaw here is the product of a woman who – and I am sorry to say this so graphically – was the product of a woman who thought she could 'turn' your father. Am I correct sir?
ALBERT *(embarrassed)* Once again, correct.
TURNER I am sorry to put this information out in the open as it where, but I believe that you were so embarrassed about your father you took on the surname of the woman who is your mother and although you tried to keep your distance from your father you followed in his footsteps and became a solicitor and four years after gaining the necessary qualifications you joined his firm, although you refused to have your name on the letterhead and worked as a junior clerk, even though you had the qualifications to branch out on your own. You only became a partner after your father died.
ALBERT Well, wouldn't you when you could earn so much money? I would have got ten percent just by law of probate, but then that blasted tape had to turn up!
TURNER Ahh yes, the tape of Henry Goodfellow's last will and testament. Thank you Albert for bringing that up; you see, on the recording that you have all heard there are many interesting sounds in the background that cannot be heard unless the sound is turned up to a level that would quite frankly be hard on the ears. The lab

boys have isolated those sounds and many of them are actually on the tape after we think the audio has finished. Glover, tape three please.

Glover refreshes the tapes and presses play. There is silence for a moment. Then we hear on the tape giggles then in the background Amanda's voice can be heard.

AMANDA *(on tape, faintly, shouting)* Alex, do you and Richard want some sandwiches and orange juice?
ALEXIS *(giggling)* Sssh! Turn that off!

Glover stops the tape. There is a moment of 'realisation' as all eyes turn to Alexis.

TURNER *(to Alexis)* Can you explain this please?
MARCUS *(stunned)* Hang on, what is that?
TURNER It is the sound of background noise after the death threat recording that was picked up by a microphone that wasn't turned off.
MARCUS *(aghast)* So are you saying that not only was the tape that I heard a fake - but it was made by my *daughter*? No way! I refuse to believe it!
TURNER I'm sorry sir, but whatever way you look at it – the recording you heard threatening you and your daughter was made by your daughter and *(checks notes)* a Richard Willoughby. You have been the victim of a prank sir.
MARCUS *(to Alexis)* I don't understand. Why? Why would you put me through such an ordeal? It, it, I just can't believe it. I'm shocked!
AMANDA *(equally shocked)* Yes, explain yourself. Why did you make such a tape?
MARCUS And how? That tape was in a sealed box. Tell me now.

Alexis's demeanour changes from a 'child' to a confident 'woman', the transformation startles everybody.

ALEXIS Well '*daddy*' it was unfortunate that these two plods found out, but I had to do it.
MARCUS *(shocked)* Why? And how?
ALEXIS Well for one you noticed the 'cheapo lock' as you called it, that was because it *was* new. The old one wasn't locked and was rusty, all I did was replace it.
MARCUS *(puzzled)* Right, okay, but I didn't ask you that, I asked you 'why'. Why did you make that recording that pretended to be my uncle Henry? Did it give you some kind of sick pleasure watching me suffer?
ALEXIS Actually it did and it worked. I needed you to be scared and also uncle Stuart to hear it because it was really aimed at him.
STUART*(Startled)* Aimed at me? Why?
ALEXIS *(amazed)* Surely you know why? How can you conveniently forget what happened that time you stayed over?
MARCUS *(confused)* What? When did you stay over? What happened?
STUART *(protesting. To Alexis)* And as I have explained a thousand times, it was a misunderstanding! I would not have said what I said if I knew it was *you* would I?

AMANDA *(alert)* What did he say?
TURNER Yes miss, what did he say to you that caused you to make that recording?
STUART *(pleading)* I really do not think that it should be out in the open Alexis, I told you until I'm blue in the face that I am sorry! Why won't you let it rest?
ALEXIS *(angry)* I can't let it rest because and you should have known better! But when you saw it was me what did you do? You just laughed and didn't do anything to make it better, did you?
STUART *(defensively)* Well if I am to blame then you are too! If I recall you didn't exactly run away crying, you took a good long look, *then* you stormed off.
AMANDA *(puzzled)* What happened between you and Stuart that upset you?
ALEXIS Well it's like this. I was desperate to use the loo and every one was being used, so I went to the guest room bathroom and Stuart was taking a shower.
STUART *(perplexed)* And what is wrong with that?
ALEXIS As soon as I went into the bathroom he pulled back the shower curtain and said 'hey, that rabbit you've just bought might like a carrot to nibble on' and he was *(she breaks down)* I'm sorry mummy, I can't. . . . . .
AMANDA *(gently coaxing)* He was what honey?
ALEXIS *(crying)* He stood there with his 'thing' pointing at me!
MARCUS/AMANDA *(shocked)* What?!
ALEXIS And he didn't cover himself up, he winked and smiled when he saw me and and he. . . . . touched himself *(sobs even louder)*
STUART *(defending himself)* That is all bollocks and she knows it! I thought it was my wife that's all!
MARCUS *(yelling he goes for Stuart)* You bloody pervert! Exposing yourself to my daughter, you git!
STUART *(hiding behind Glover)* I am not a pervert! I was having a shower, did you think I would be wearing a Mackintosh or something?! I thought it was my wife, I really did! She's the pervert, she tried to knock my hand away so she could get a 'better look'. I did nothing wrong, I was just having a shower!
AMANDA *(angry)* Really? It all fits now why you haven't been here that often in the last ten months.
STUART *(raising his voice)* Well maybe that is because of your sex mad daughter! *She* was the one who came into the bathroom and pulled the shower curtain back and that is the truth! I didn't do *anything*, but she paints the picture of innocence, which she isn't! I know you and that Richard lad had been having under age sex because he told me when he got got a bit drunk at that gig we went to when we all saw that so called Beatles "tribute act"!
ALEXIS *(lying)* No we didn't! It's a lie!
STUART *(angrily)* Is it? He couldn't wait to tell me! He was so smug about it I wanted to punch his face in!
AMANDA *(interrupting)* Hang on, when was this?
STUART February last year.
AMANDA *(to Alexis)* You were fifteen February last year.
STUART *(triumphant)* Exactly!
AMANDA *(annoyed)* I will deal with you later young lady!

ALEXIS *(protesting)* Uncle Stuart is lying mummy!
AMANDA Is he? I don't think so. *(to Stuart)* If you knew all of this then why didn't you say something to me?
STUART How could I?!
ALEXIS He couldn't say anything because he's making it all up!
STUART Oh stop trying to deny it! Why I am being made to look like a pervy villain is just stupid! Have you ever been in her bedroom? If you do you will find the stash of "Hustler" magazines in the box under her window. Oh, surprised are we Alex? You may be "nearly eighteen" but Richard is nineteen, he told me he buys them for you and don't deny it!
ALEXIS *(embarrassed)* Have you been in my bedroom?
STUART No I haven't. Your boyfriend also told me all about them. He says that you are a quite a "rampant little minx" and that you "can't get enough". So don't blame me for what *you* are like. And what you did when I was taking a shower is more your fault than mine!
ALEXIS *(unrepentant)* So?! Looking at pictures isn't the same as it actually being there in front of you is it?
STUART *(sarcastically)* And that is your defence is it?
MARCUS I think it's a perfectly good one! How could you Stuart? First you are always playing squash with my wife and then you try it on with my daughter! This is partly why we haven't spoken for eight years it's because you mock me constantly!
STUART *(amazed)* Really? So you think that I 'exposed myself' to your daughter to 'mock' you even more, is that it? Have you any idea what that sounds like? You should be asking her why she made that tape!
ALEXIS I made that tape to get revenge on you! The last time you came here it was my birthday and you didn't speak to me, you ignored me and that annoyed me a lot. Especially when you just handed me a birthday card with ten pounds in it like I was a child or something. Ten pounds! Am I not worth more to you than that? You promised me driving lessons and I never got them. And you left the price sticker on the card; eighty nine pence! And then you left after an hour. I was very upset and you didn't care! *(she begins to sob)*

There is a stand-off, everybody calms down.

TURNER *(delicately)* Well miss, you have a lot of questions to answer. The first one being why did you made that tape?
ALEXIS *(sobbing)* It was meant to be a joke. I didn't think that he *(points at Albert)* would phone the police, or that father would take it so seriously. But after what Stuart did to me I wanted revenge, it's as simple as that. I just wanted to frighten them both that's all.
STUART And as I have told you many times since, I thought you were my wife!
ALEXIS *(ignores him)* Anyway, mister Forshaw came here with the box of tapes and dad wouldn't open it. So when he was out I thought I'd have a nosey and when I tried the lock it literally broke off when I touched it. Anyway, I opened it and was disappointed to see all those tapes, but on the top was the one with dads name on it.

So I played it and it was the recording of the will. But I was still annoyed at uncle Stuart because he came round a few days before and he still ignored me. So I asked Richard to pretend to be Henry and he did the voices heard on that tape. I did it to scare daddy and piss off Stuart. It was only meant to be a joke, I didn't think it would go this far, I really didn't, but that's all it ever was *meant* to be – a joke. I wanted daddy to be pleased that Richard could do a voice that sounded like his dead uncle, I didn't know he and him *(points at Forshaw)* would take it so seriously. Surely you could have guessed it was a joke dad.

MARCUS *(embarrassed)* Well no, I didn't think it was a joke and Albert acted on it with considerable efficiency if I may say so. But making that tape and pretending that we are in jeopardy wasn't funny! And for what? So you could get a barmy revenge on your uncle Stuart? The mind boggles I can tell you!

TURNER You may have made the tape as a joke miss, but it doesn't really explain why mister Forshaw rang us does it?

ALBERT You know why I rang you, there was a death threat on the tape, I had to presume that it was genuine that is all.

TURNER No you didn't, it was because you knew it wasn't a real tape as you never lost the written version of the will did you as it wasn't 'lost' in the first place was it?

ALBERT *(bluffing)* I don't know what you mean.

TURNER You know exactly what I mean. A written copy was made and most probably typed up and signed by Henry Goodfellow and Michael Stevens, it is a standard procedure. As far as we know there hasn't been an updated will. You have deliberately mislaid the written will because it contradicts what was heard on the recording that threatened mister Winstanley; but as we have just heard, the recording that was made then has to be considered as the last true will mister Henry Goodfellow made. So, what have you got to hide?

ALBERT *(bluffing)* I did not know that the recording I heard was a fake. But as a precaution, I went back to the office and removed anything concerning Henry Goodfellow in case you came snooping around and found something that you could consider 'evidence'. But as you have already discovered; Michael Stevens was my father. *(defeated)* Well, it all seems so pointless now.

STUART Hang on here, am I going loopy or what? Aren't we missing something here?

GLOVER And what would that be sir?

STUART If the "Will" stipulated that everything was to go to Michael Stevens, who is now dead, then in effect everything now goes to his direct heir - Albert Forshaw; Who is the son of a gay. You lucky guy!

ALBERT *(proudly)* Why thank you sir.

MARCUS *(protesting)* Hang on! Why should he get all that money? And why didn't uncle Henry change his will? This is too stupid for words it really is!

AMANDA Oh shut up will you! Until two weeks ago you weren't bothered about money, your wallet is so full of dead moths there isn't any room for putting notes in! So forget all about it and for once think of your family and put all your energy into keeping *us* happy. Is that too much to ask?

MARCUS I always think of you and Alexis. Why do you think I work so hard!

AMANDA That's all well and good, but we never see any of your hard work. When was the last holiday we took as a family? Go on, I'd love to know. *(no response)* You can't remember can you? Well I will tell you; it was two years ago! *Two*! And then it was to Bloody Butlins. That stupid eighties weekend with bands that even I can't remember!
MARCUS *(amazed)* And what's wrong with Butlins?
AMANDA Nothing in summer; but this was the end of *October*!
TURNER *(interrupts)* If you don't mind, I think we are straying off a tangent here. Obviously there are many issues and resentments in your family relationships that go back many years, but as far as we are concerned that is not our business and we do not wish to get involved; but there is still a factor in this case that hasn't been brought to your attention and it is a most important one at that.
STUART Oh? And what would that be?
TURNER It is Mr Forshaws relationship with your uncle sir.
STUART We know that, he was his solicitor and just happens to be a bastard just like myself and Marcus.
TURNER Either you chose to ignore what I have just said or you have misheard what I have just said.
STUART I heard what you said.
ALBERT *(cutting in)* No you didn't, you don't understand do you? You are indeed correct in saying that as I am the 'bastard' child of Michael Stevens and that everything in the will does go to me, but I am going to confess that for the last five years of Henry's life he and I had a 'special' relationship that went beyond money or anything else for that matter.

Confused pause, Alexis breaks it.

ALEXIS *(scoffing)* Where you and Henry giving each other one?
ALBERT *(embarrassed)* Well I wouldn't put it so crudely, but we were very intimate certainly. And I am not a homosexual, despite what this all looks like.
MARCUS *(stunned)* Really?
ALBERT When I say 'very intimate' I don't mean it in the way you think. Your uncle Henry and I had got to be very close in his last few years and he often spoke of how his only two nephews ignored him and let him rot away. Stuart had visited him many times as indeed you did, but not as often in his later years because, by your own admissions you "couldn't bear the smell" and also the fact that you really wanted to disown him. But that was before you knew how much he was worth and that is when your daughter and I planned to get revenge as a way of humiliating you both.
MARCUS *(aghast)* Pardon? Are you saying that my daughter and *you* planned this whole 'death threat' nonsense? Why?

There are looks of "accusations" towards each other. Finally Alexis breaks the tension.

ALEXIS I'll tell you father. I have a box full of letters that your uncle Henry wrote to

you in the last years of his life that you tore up and binned. I saved them all and I was disgusted at the attitude you had towards him. He was reaching out to you to make peace and you chose to ignore them. That is when Albert and I came up with the idea of the false tape. But I wasn't counting on the police being so efficient and discovering the original recording under the one Richard made and then recording mum shouting us down for lunch. But what can I do, it's all out in the open now and you have lost out to fourteen million pounds.
MARCUS *(staggered)* I can't believe it. My own daughter conspiring against me. *(to Amanda)* I suppose you were in on this charade too?
AMANDA *(outraged)* Don't look at me, I'm just as shocked as you are.
MARCUS *(scoffing)* Really? Well I don't know what to think. You have all been devious and conspired against me, what the hell am I supposed to do now. Disown my daughter? Disown my wife? This is all so ridiculous for words. I wouldn't be surprised if you two plods are in on it!
TURNER *(surprised)* I can assure you that we are not involved. But at least I can say that I have a 'solved case' and that the threat of mine and Glovers demotion has been lifted. I must say that this not only has been my quickest case, but the most satisfying and I thank you for giving me the opportunity I really do.
MARCUS *(aghast)* Well that is all well and good. But surely Albert and Alexis should be arrested and charged with forgery or something? They shouldn't be allowed to get away with what they have done!
TURNER Well sir, I would say that you have been the victim of a practical joke and technically they haven't done anything except give your brother a bloody nose and you a lesson in family unity. Not to mention that money isn't always the be all and end all. As far as Glover and I am concerned the case is closed and you can squabble as much as you like. So if you will excuse us.
MARCUS *(amazed)* Surely they must be guilty of doing something? Isn't making false death threats against the law or something?
TURNER As I said before sir, all it looks like from a police point of view is that you have been the victim of a practical joke and that there is no case to answer. Goodnight everybody. Glover.
GLOVER Goodnight sir.

They collect their things as everybody looks on amazed, Marcus tries to stop them, but to no avail, they exit.

MARCUS Hang on! Is that it? Shouldn't they be charged with forgery or something? *(they have exited, he throws his hands up in defeat)* I don't believe this! This is all beyond a joke, it really is!! Well, that wasn't what I expected and especially from you, young lady! *(flustered)* Why? Why would you do it you little . . . . .
STUART *(amused)* I do believe Marcus is going to swear! That's a first!
MARCUS *(angrily)* Oh shut up you sarcastic git!

END OF SCENE TWO

SCENE THREE immediately after.

Everybody is tense, Marcus is pacing the room, giving Alexis evil looks as she sits with a serene expression.

MARCUS *(to Alexis, sternly)* So young lady, what was with the tape that you say is a 'joke'? Why would you do such a thing to me? To us? Your mother and I had been through a lot of stress over what you have done.
AMANDA *(surprised)* Me? No, not really.
MARCUS Why? Where you in on the 'joke' as well? Weren't you concerned for me?
AMANDA Actually, no I wasn't. But why should I have been concerned when you are hardly home? Many times I think I do not know you and that's your fault not being home, not being here for Alexis and I. But admittedly at the back of my mind I knew you would be okay. And it was a very clever 'joke' by Alex I must say.
ALEXIS *(proudly)* Thank you mother.
AMANDA Credit where it's due sweetie. You have certainly woken your father up to his lack of awareness of his family obligations. I have a sneaky idea that that was your intention in the first place. Am I right?
ALEXIS Actually mother I just wanted to wake him up and realise that we are here as he never notices you or me. Plus I was very upset that he always forgot about Richard whenever I spoke of him. I speak of him all the time and you don't listen do you?
MARCUS *(sarcastic, rubs his eyes)* Awe, boo hoo. I am always at work or away, why should your so called 'boyfriend' be of interest to me? Have I met him?
ALEXIS *(annoyed)* I have known him for three years and we are actually going to get engaged on my eighteenth birthday! But you don't even know he exists and how do you think I feel about that?!
MARCUS Well I feel that you are very annoyed, I can see that. But how the hell did you manage to make that recording that fooled Stuart here?
STUART I would rather be a fool than an idiot who's family resort to desperate measures to get them to notice you. You are your own worst enemy you know.
MARCUS *(angrily)* Oh shut up! Who ask you to speak?
ALEXIS Uncle Stuart is right dad. I am sorry that I did what I did to you and to Stuart, but if it makes you be the father that I wish to have then I hope you will forgive me?
MARCUS *(aghast)* Forgive you? Why would I want to do that? You got your future 'husband' to imitate my dead uncle and make that false recorded will. Did it give you some kind of amusement?
ALEXIS Of course it did! I told you Richard can do impressions of people loads of times and you ignored me and then went off on another jaunt abroad somewhere. It was if I was just 'there', like a pet. Anyway, when you got that box of tapes off your uncle Henry and I saw the one that had your name on it; well I played it and I couldn't

believe it. So I asked Richard to listen to it and have a go of imitating Henry's voice. I wrote out what I wanted him to say and he pretended to be both the voices you heard and the one you didn't. He did a good job don't you think? It was a bit over the top, but I thought it was funny watching you squirm.
MARCUS Well 'ha ha'. Very funny I must say and to be honest – I am impressed. In fact, not only am I impressed, but you actually managed to prise some money out of me for a horse. *(hugs her)* You devious little cow!
ALEXIS *(proudly)* Thank you daddy.
MARCUS And stop calling me daddy, you are nearly eighteen!
ALEXIS *(happy)* Of course I will. . . . .daddy.
MARCUS *(impressed)* So you made a recording, put on a new lock, that I didn't think anything of and got money out of me. Very clever. But what I haven't figured out is why would uncle Henry leave me that box of jazz tapes and one of them was so blatantly made out to me? That is what I find so strange and one that the police should have been asking questions about.

Everybody shrugs, Albert nervously shifts from foot to foot. Marcus notices.

You have turned a little uneasy Albert, is there something you might like to tell me?
ALBERT *(uneasy)* I do not know what you are talking about. I'm just tired that's all, it has been very stressful all this business with the tape.
MARCUS *(suspiciously)* Really? Now I come to think of it; I did think it odd that out of all those tapes in that box there was one tape that had my name on it. It was a box that you gave to me claiming to be from uncle Henry.

Albert looks increasingly uncomfortable.

I think there is something that is making Albert nervous. What is it?
ALBERT *(nervously)* Nothing. It's just hot in here that's all.
STUART You are sweating rather profusely I must say. Wouldn't you say so ladies?
AMANDA I do. If I didn't know better I would say Albert either has something to hide or is worried that something might be found out. Am I correct?
ALBERT Nonsense! I'm just warm that's all. Now, if you don't mind I am leaving as there is nothing more to be said about the will. It is obviously void and the will is now a ward of the state until it can be determined who it should go to. Goodnight.

He makes his way to the door, Marcus blocks him.

MARCUS Sorry old chap, but you are not leaving here until you explain your 'special relationship' with uncle Henry.
STUART We know his 'special relationship' though don't we? He almost confessed it. He was "boffin" uncle Henry, weren't you?
ALBERT *(disgusted)* Do you have to put it so uncouthly?
STUART *(innocently)* What other way would you put it?
ALBERT Not quite like that sir. It's true that your uncle Henry and I had a very close

relationship; especially during the last years of his life. But we were not 'boffin' each other as you so crudely put it.
MARCUS *(surprised)* Really? You and my daughter conspire to make a tape that says I will die if I don't marry a woman named Amanda or have a male child and you claim that *nothing* went on between you and uncle Henry, yet you, as the only child of Michael Stevens inherits *every* penny? Well unless I'm wrong please explain what is really going on. After all, I have nothing to lose now and you have fourteen million reasons to put the matter straight.
ALBERT *(resigned)* Alright, if you want to hear it, then you had better sit down. There was no tape. It was all a joke.

Everybody is stunned at this news and murmur loudly, Albert calms everybody down. They become silent and listen.

The original recording that the police found was actually a recording of me doing both voices. It wasn't meant to have been recorded over, the original intention was to make an 'updated will' on the reverse that your daughter's boyfriend was to make. But the idiot recorded over the one that I made, so what could I do?
ALEXIS *(annoyed)* Don't blame Richard, you should have rewound the tape so we knew which side to record on!
ALBERT *(embarrassed)* I know that! I rewound the wrong side. Anyway, the two recordings were made, I placed the tape in the box with all the others and gave it to you. And the rest you know.
MARCUS *(stunned)* But *why*? Did I upset you in anyway?
ALBERT No sir, you didn't. I had to do what I did, because uncle Henry never made a will. All his estate, by law, goes to any surviving relatives that he has.

There is a silence as everybody ponders what Albert has said.

STUART *(realising)* That's Marcus and me!
ALBERT Correct sir.
MARCUS *(puzzled)* Hang on. If you knew of this then why did you phone the police up in the first place?
ALBERT To add credibility should it ever be contested in court.
MARCUS *(surprised)* Eh?
ALBERT It's quite simple sir and I have already told you. I looked after your uncle Henry for many years before he died and he would never make a will, even though he promised me that he would. Your uncle Henry and I even had a 'civil wedding' with the intention of making me his "legal heir", but after his death, it was never acknowledged in court as I was not considered by the court to be a "legal heir" and also I wasn't a direct 'bloodline'. And just to remind you all, I am not a homosexual, it was a "marriage of convenience" to stop you two from gaining something that you did not deserve, that's all.
AMANDA I agree, these two need a kick up the bum. Good plan Albert.
ALBERT Thank you Mrs Winstanley.

AMANDA Amanda, just call me Amanda, stop being so formal will you.
ALBERT Of course, sorry, Amanda.
AMANDA That's better.
MARCUS Whoa, rewind a bit. You and uncle Henry got *married?*
ALBERT *(embarrassed)* Correct sir.
MARCUS *(amazed)* I don't understand You got married just so you could inherit his wealth? Don't you think that's a bit devious? Is it legal in this country?
ALBERT Maybe and possibly and it's up to the courts. *(he is becoming angry)* But look at it from my point of view. Why should you two gain when you didn't care for him? I cleaned up his mess, I did everything for him and neither of you cared for him, or bothered with him or ever visited or enquired to his health in his last few years and what did I get in return for my looking after him when he died? Nothing.

Everybody sits in stunned silence for a minute.

MARCUS *(finally)* Well Albert, I am so sorry that you have been treated so shabbily and I congratulate you on the ingenious tape, also my daughter too. Genius, absolutely genius I must say.

He moves to the drinks cabinet, pours himself a drink and ponders. Amanda is impatient.

AMANDA Here we go! There is something of an idea forming in that pea of a brain isn't there?
MARCUS *(proudly)* There certainly is!
AMANDA Well come on!
MARCUS Okay, this is how I see it. Uncle Henry never made a recording of his will, Stuart and I are the only surviving family legally entitled to Henry's estate. So, what I propose is this: Stuart gets two million, I get five million.
STUART *(protesting)* Hang on, why should I get two million and you five?

Everybody murmurs their unhappiness at this news.

MARCUS *(gesturing for quiet)* Hang on, hang on! Please let me explain if that is alright, please?

The murmurs cease.

Thank you. I think it's fair, as it was me who was "threatened", albeit a forgery. Let's say it's "compensation" for the stress I've endured over the last few weeks shall we?
STUART *(shrugging)* Fair enough, I can't argue with two million.
MARCUS Good. Now Albert also gets two million, would you say that is fair for all your troubles and looking after Henry?
ALBERT *(flattered)* More than enough sir. Thank you. *(uncertain)* But are you sure sir? It is rather a lot of money.

MARCUS Albert, if you do not accept it then I will share it out between my wife and Alexis. That money should more than adequately compensate you for all your care of uncle Henry. Is that clear?
ALBERT Perfectly sir.
MARCUS Good. The remaining money will be divided thus, Amanda will receive three million and Alexis one million, with an increase of another two million on your twenty first birthday. How does that sound? Am I being fair everybody?

Murmurs of "yes", I suppose so", wow" etc.

The only other area of Henry's none "will" that needs to be sorted are his stocks and shares, effects, properties and art collection. As I do not know whereabouts he owned them Albert and I will sort that out another day. But is everybody happy with what they've got?

Murmurs of "more than", "thank you", "very generous" etc.

Good. Alexis has more than enough money to have an engagement party and I am very certain one of uncle Henry's properties would make a fine house for you; though I must stipulate that the house goes into your name only should you ever get divorced. Is that okay with you sweetie?
ALEXIS *(pleased)* More than fair and extremely generous of you father. Thank you *(she hugs him)*.
MARCUS *(with humour)* Now now Alex, you will have me blushing! So everybody is happy with the way I have shared the money? *(with obvious relish)* Especially Stuart who now has money to help him pay for those Thai prostitutes that he doesn't know that I know about! *(Stuart looks horrified, Marcus laughs)* Only joking Stuart! And Amanda can finally pay off her credit card bill, yay! So everyone's a winner!
STUART *(stunned, taking Marcus to one side)* How did you know about Thailand?
MARCUS *(turning his back to everybody: quietly)* Simple. We stayed in the same hotel once last year when I was there on a state visit, you were most likely selling your tractor parts to poor farmers. What date was it? Hmm, let me think. . . . October fourteenth I think it was. I'm surprised that you didn't know I was there? *(Stuart looks blank, Marcus is amazed)* Surely you must have known about the state visit? It was all over the television? No? I was amazed at your blatant cheek, surely you would have known you would be spotted? Anyway, I saw you register at reception, but thankfully you didn't see me. About two days later I saw you take a 'lady' to your room and I *knew* the lady in question because she tried it on with me when I arrived. Don't worry, I won't tell your wife about your shenanigans, *(with menace)* only if you promise to keep your shower sessions behind locked doors should you ever stay in this house again while I am away. Is that understood?
STUART *(understanding)* Perfectly.
MARCUS Good. Because if you *ever* take a shower knowing my daughter – or my wife is near, then I will not hesitate in showing your wife the video of you and "Chloe", oh *and* "Amy" making out in the hotel bar. Do you understand?

STUART *(worried)* Did you make a recording?
MARCUS *(evilly)* Oh yes, *(produces his phone)* on my phone. Technology these days is amazing, don't you think?
STUART *(beat, contrite)* Obviously I do not have a choice.
MARCUS Good. I am so glad we understand each other. *(holds out his hand)* Shake on it? And by the way, I have made a recording of the night. Or three; just in case you think of stealing my phone. You see, you may think that you are smart because you know so much about me, even though we haven't seen each other in eight years; but that is nothing to what I know about you and what it could do to your marriage; should the recording ever get "accidentally" posted to your "drop dead gorgeous wife". *(Stuart is stunned and ashen faced)* Not bad for someone who is "boring as hell", is it? Good lad, I am glad we "understand" each other *(Stuart numbly shakes his hand. Marcus pats him very hard on the back)* Excellent! *(flamboyantly).* Well everybody we're all richer than we were yesterday and that is because my devious daughter and Albert each made a false tape. Genius I must say. So, let's have a toast. *(surprised)* No drinks? Amanda, will you do the honours please, thank you.

Amanda pours out five glasses of sherry and hands them out.

In the last couple of weeks I have been exposed as a non-caring tight wad and been shown the error of my ways. I hope the money you have been given a share of is a start of a new me and that I will continue to be more generous in the future and if I am not, then you will endeavour to make sure I get back on track. So everybody, raise your glasses for uncle Henry.

They all raise their glasses and toast uncle Henry.

ALBERT *(embarrassed)* Er, sorry to bring this up, but do not forget that inheritance tax duties must be paid, also Death Duties and also the "gift tax" on your uncle Henry's properties and effects, plus solicitor fees and burial costs .
MARCUS *(annoyed)* Oh bloody hell Albert, did you have to bring that up!
ALBERT *(embarrassed)* Sorry sir, it is the law you know.
MARCUS Bugger!
AMANDA *(Cheerfully)* Oh come on darling, it's not the end of the world you know. Your six million will still be worth around five after taxes and I do rather like that house he had in Cannes, plus now that we are now enormously wealthy we can *(whispers in his ear)*
MARCUS *(shocked)* Amanda! Why you . . . . . though come to think of it it has been a dream of mine. I will take some more overdue leave and maybe we could *(whispers in her ear, she is shocked)* Come on everybody *(raises his glass)* To uncle Henry, the richest dead man I never knew. Cheers.
ALL Cheers to uncle Henry – hurrah!!

They all "toast" Uncle Henry.

THE END.

About the play

Hello reader.

I hope you have enjoyed this story of an intriguing situation regarding a deceased man's Will and the circumstances that surround it. The idea behind it was a simple one about a person receiving a "death threat" through a deceased relative on a cassette that accurately predicted that threatened person's life; even though the cassette was dated over 25 years previously. It was an intriguing idea that I had way back sometime in 1992! Yep, a long long time ago to be sure.

So with that simple premise I set about writing the play in October 2011, spread over ten evenings over two separate weeks (either side of a week of working till way past 8 o'clock PM) and I got the first draft quickly down in that time. Probably one of the quickest plays I have ever written! (as in typed up) I didn't know where I was going with the play, I made it up as I went along, having no "plan" for it, but it kept me on my toes I must say.

I published the script as a FIRST DRAFT! Yes, *that is right*, a first draft! I did state that it would be limited to 25 copies only in the original draft, but in the end, it was only 12 copies, (I did give it a lot of thought and well, 12 copies does make it a very rare collector's item should I ever make it as a writer). The first draft contained many spelling mistakes, continuity errors and plot details that didn't sit well on the first reading. But I was so impressed with my own writing that I was prepared to publish this play (errors included etc.) because I was so knocked out with what I had written. It was not something that I would usually do, but hey, "when in Rome" etc. . . . Also, you will notice that I have a fixation with being rude! I can't help it, it's just how my mind was working when I wrote this. So if you do not like the shocking "Reveal" (followed by yet another shocking "Reveal"), then maybe this play isn't for you! But the play wouldn't work without a bit of "rude" in it. Oh well, I can't please everybody.

Since the publication of the "first draft" I have added many pages of dialogue and also cut out dialogue that was considered "unnecessary" and yet, the play could be vastly different once it ever becomes a "staged play" and I know the facts regarding Wills and the ways the Police operate (although from feedback, the "facts" do not matter as the play "works" as it is)

As I always say - "enjoy", and if you want to leave me a suggestion about where the play can be "tweaked" or "altered", or just downright incorrect, then please email me at robbiegood@hotmail.com or robthewriter@hotmail.co.uk and put in the subject box "Will Play", should it go into my "junk box". Thank you.

Robert Goodier (November 2012)

Other plays by the author

TO BE ANNOUNCED

Ever wondered how a successful Amateur Dramatics Society is run? Who casts the parts and selects the seasons plays? Well this hilarious play takes you behinds the scenes of a squabbling society with two of the main protagonists fighting it out to be the head honcho.

Alice is opposed to Maggie, who for years has been trying to persuade her society to stage one of the many plays that she's written, but Alice is Chairwoman and has the final say; which is always 'No'. Matters come to a head after a heated argument, in which Maggie is booted from the society and out of spite they both stage a play at the same time in a battle of supremacy. Who wins? The audience does! So come along, buy a front row seat and take a peek inside as the battle rages.

MURDEROUS INTENTIONS

Alistair and Martine Richmond live in their sprawling country mansion near Chorley Lancashire and have buried their daughter who had drowned two weeks before. On the night of the funeral strange things happen to the housekeeper in the kitchen and who is the mysterious figure in the grounds looking at the house? And why has Charles Richmond been locked in his suddenly freezing Arctic bedroom for the night? The next day all is revealed by an unexpected visitor. . . . who reveals secrets the Richmond family desperately tried to hide from each other and changes their lives. Forever.

GHOST OF THORNLEY HALL IN CUMBRIA

Retired Detective Inspector Mr. Armani and his wife are invited by a long forgotten relative to stay the weekend at his Cumbrian mansion for the reading of a will, he is not expecting the 'eccentricities' of the relatives and other guests. Nor is he expecting the tale of a ghost of the first Earl of Thornley to be so prominent. But it is the three hundredth anniversary of his death and his ghost still haunts the house! Mr. Armani is in no mood for the hidden treasure or the attempts to find it. Neither is he in the mood for Timpkins the frustrated and annoying butler, Edna the maid who will 'dress up' for the Earl, Mabel the sex mad niece, Kipling the dodgy tenant or the Winsomes or Winthorp, the Earls devious valet. In fact he wants to relax, but everybody - and his wife - have different ideas!

ROBBIE NUDD AND THE MAGNIFICENT SEVEN.

A PANTOMIME

Robbie Nudds merry men have been kidnapped by the evil Madoona who has plans for them to dance on her world tour and video for her latest single. Luckily the Sherf of Knottyham is distracted by a visit by his wife's relatives and can't be bothered to hound Robbie for taxes. Robbie 'borrows' the Sherfs' nephews and nieces in his quest to rescue his merry men, walking for miles through fields, over mountains, taking in the sights of London and the pub.

Whilst on their travels a man who calls himself Prince and is a mean sword fighter, is lost on his way to Knottyham on his quest to see the evil Sherf. The mission Prince is on requires the Sherf's arrest for non-payment of taxes.

When Robbie and the gang find Madoona's lair and rescue the merry men they return to Knottyham and persuade Prince not to have the Sherf hanged - even though no-one can stand him. It is then discovered that the Sherf is his father and they are reunited. It also turns out that there is no tour, it was just a trick to get Robbie there so Madoona can enslave him as her husband. Obviously Robbie isn't pleased about being enslaved and kidnaps Madoona himself to take back to Knottyham where she falls head over heels in love with Prince. Prince forgives the Sherf for abandoning him and offers to put him up in London to stay for the rest of his life. So everybody is reunited and lives happily ever after.

ANDREW BOAR: SPECIAL AGENT

A spoof play set in 1997 that has no relevance to world events whatsoever!

Andrew Boar faces his most dangerous assignment as he races against time to discover why the Vodka supplied from Russia has been contaminated with a hormone replacement that turns men into women and women into men, almost instantly. His assignment takes him around the world and when he discovers the mad men behind the evil plot he is shocked to the core! Who is behind the mad scheme to poison the worlds vodka? You will have to join him on his assignment to find out!

BEHIND ENEMY LINES

(TOP SECRET! EYES ONLY!)

A war time play set in a World War that took place between 1939 and 1945. The subject is top secret, but it involves Corporal Jennifer Saunders infiltrating Hitler's Third Reich with the mission being life and death, possibly Hitler's or her own. Join her on her mission to find out. Debriefing over.

PERFECT SUSPECT

Marcus Winstanley inherits a vast fortune from an extremely rich uncle and while going through his uncles possessions he finds a cassette tape in a locked case with his name on it, dated 25 years previous. Curious, he listens to the tape to discover that his uncle was talking to another man about having him killed should he not get married or if he did his wife did not bear him a son. This completely stuns him, as the tape also states the name of his wife *and* the name of his daughter and also a *date* on which he would be murdered by the mystery man on the tape. The news upsets him and Police Inspectors Turner and Glover do not reassure him with their confidence either! Not only that, but the news of the Will also upsets his brother, who tended to his uncle in his last years and he is annoyed that he doesn't get a penny *and* add to the fact that the recording of his dead uncle's Will states that Marcus has two weeks left to live; the race is on to halt his ultimate demise!

FAMILY REVELATIONS

Maureen Jackman is a tyrant, she rules over her ex bank robbing husband Colin with a hard fist and takes no nonsense from her son Leonard who she thinks is going to get engaged to the daughter of the richest family In town. But at a party that she insists on having, she meets Leonard's bride to be and her family. Their eccentric lifestyle opens her eyes, making her realise that being an old 'fuddy duddy' is out of sorts with the world as she realises her son isn't the man she thought she was.

www.ingramcontent.com/pod-product-compliance
Ingram Content Group UK Ltd.
Pitfield, Milton Keynes, MK11 3LW, UK
UKHW020234250726
13967UKWH00001B/365

9 781471 766725